KU-059-531

Understanding

CORONARY
HEART DISEASE

Dr Chris Davidson

Published by Family Doctor Publications Limited
in association with the British Medical Association

Family Doctor Publications, PO Box 4664, Poole BH15 1NN

Medical Editor: Dr Tony Smith
Consultant Editors: Chris McLaughlin and Sue Davidson
Cover Artist: Dave Eastbury
Illustrator: Passmore Technical Art Services
Medical Artist: Gillian Lee
Design: MPG Design, Blandford Forum, Dorset
Printing: Reflex Litho, Thetford, Norfolk, using acid-free paper

ISBN: 1 898205 71 X

Contents

Introduction

This book is about coronary heart disease, or CHD for short. The word coronary refers to the coronary arteries, the small blood vessels that keep the heart muscle supplied with the oxygen and nutrients that it needs to work properly.

Changes in the coronary arteries build up over many years, and can lead to angina, heart attacks and sudden death. Indeed CHD is the single most common cause of death in the UK (see figure on page 3). Most people will know someone who has had a heart attack, often without any warning, but this was not always so.

CHD has become more common over the last 50 years, and we know some of the important factors responsible for the increase. This booklet aims to tell you more about this condition, what to do if you have it, and what you can do to prevent it.

WHAT'S IN A NAME?

There are several terms used to describe coronary disease and its effects on the heart. Coronary heart disease (CHD) is the one used in this book, but others you may hear doctors use are shown in the box.

CAD – coronary artery disease	Disease of the coronary arteries themselves
IHD – ischaemic heart disease	Narrowing of the blood vessels results in ischaemia, that is, lack of blood supply to the heart muscle

MI – myocardial infarction
  – coronary, coronary thrombosis
  – heart attack
	Death of an area of heart muscle as a result of blockage in blood supply

Coronary artery disease can cause a range of different problems, all resulting from insufficient oxygen reaching the heart muscle. The most common of them are:

- Angina – chest pain when exercising; this can include everyday physical effort, not just activities such as aerobics or jogging! The pain gets better when you rest.

- Heart attack (MI) – death of an area of heart muscle when the blood supply is cut off completely giving severe chest pain.

The following are other conditions that are often the result of coronary heart disease:

- Heart failure – in which the heart cannot pump well enough to keep up with the body's demands, leading to breathlessness and swollen ankles.

- Irregularities of heart rhythm (arrhythmias) – irregular beats which can cause palpitations and breathlessness.

Not all heart disease is coronary artery disease, but it is far and away the most common cause. Other heart problems include:

- Congenital heart disease – abnormalities of the heart which are present at birth, such as hole in the heart.

- Cardiomyopathies – diseases that primarily affect the heart muscle rather than the arteries.

- Valvular heart disease – damage to or abnormalities of any of the four valves that control blood flow in the heart.

WHO GETS HEART DISEASE?

The number of people who get coronary heart disease varies enormously from one country to another. We are all used to the idea that certain diseases are common in some countries but not others, yet we don't usually see our own country in the same way. But if we were looking down on the Earth from another planet we would be as struck by the very high rates of heart disease in the British Isles as we might be by malaria in the tropics. Unfortunately, in the UK we are among the worst in the world league table, which is something that, as a nation, we cannot ignore.

In general, CHD is a disease of affluence. It is becoming more common in developing countries, but is most common in northern Europe, North America and Australasia. It does seem to be related in some way to lifestyle, because when people move from

DEATHS BY CAUSE, MEN AND WOMEN UNDER 75

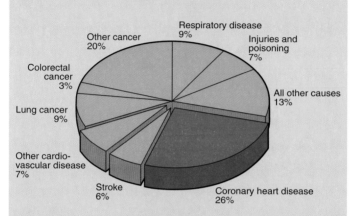

UK men 2001

Respiratory disease
9%

Injuries and poisoning
7%

Other cancer
20%

Colorectal cancer
3%

All other causes
13%

Lung cancer
9%

Other cardio-vascular disease
7%

Stroke
6%

Coronary heart disease
26%

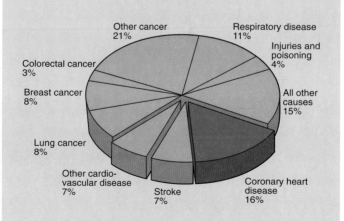

UK women 2001

Other cancer
21%

Respiratory disease
11%

Injuries and poisoning
4%

Colorectal cancer
3%

Breast cancer
8%

All other causes
15%

Lung cancer
8%

Other cardio-vascular disease
7%

Stroke
7%

Coronary heart disease
16%

Source: British Heart Foundation Statistics Database, 2001.

DEATH RATE FROM CHD BY AREA

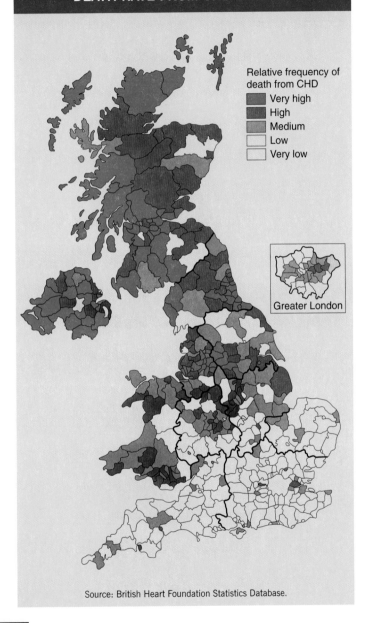

Relative frequency of death from CHD

- Very high
- High
- Medium
- Low
- Very low

Greater London

Source: British Heart Foundation Statistics Database.

the developing countries to a more affluent culture they get CHD much more often than they would have done at home. This is particularly noticeable among immigrants from the Indian subcontinent who come to the UK and who are then even more likely to develop CHD than people who were born here.

Within Europe there are major differences between countries and even within one country. In southern Europe, CHD is generally much less common than in the UK and Scandinavia – one of the reasons for the popularity of the Mediterranean diet at present. Many people believe that this way of eating – with lots of fresh vegetables, salad, fruit and fish and relatively little red meat or dairy produce – can help protect against heart disease (more about this on pages 69–72). In the UK itself there are also large variations between regions; the highest rates are in what were the old areas of industrialisation – northern England, Scotland, Wales and Northern Ireland.

Although descriptions of CHD date back to the classical world, it was not recognised to be a common disease until after World War II. The rate of heart disease, particularly among young men, rose

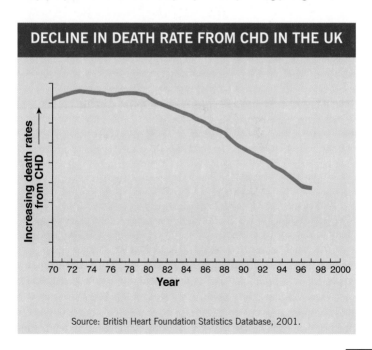

DECLINE IN DEATH RATE FROM CHD IN THE UK

Increasing death rates from CHD →

70 72 74 76 78 80 82 84 86 88 90 92 94 96 98 2000
Year

Source: British Heart Foundation Statistics Database, 2001.

INCIDENCE OF CHD IN EUROPE

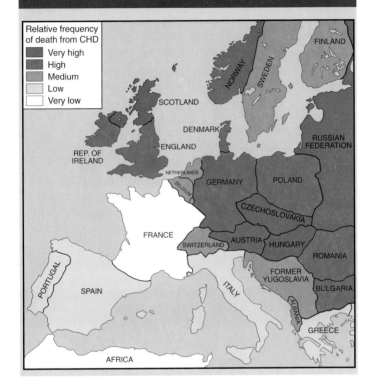

Relative frequency of death from CHD

- Very high
- High
- Medium
- Low
- Very low

FINLAND
NORWAY
SWEDEN
SCOTLAND
DENMARK
RUSSIAN FEDERATION
ENGLAND
REP. OF IRELAND
NETHERLANDS
BELGIUM
GERMANY
POLAND
CZECHOSLOVAKIA
FRANCE
SWITZERLAND
AUSTRIA
HUNGARY
ROMANIA
FORMER YUGOSLAVIA
PORTUGAL
ITALY
BULGARIA
SPAIN
ALBANIA
GREECE
AFRICA

alarmingly, but peaked in the USA and Australia in 1970 and has been falling steadily ever since. In the UK too, the rates of CHD have been declining slowly since 1980. Unfortunately, rates are rising rapidly in eastern Europe, with countries such as Russia and the Baltic states now heading the league table.

It is no exaggeration to say that most hospital beds in the UK are occupied by people whose illness is in some way related to hardening of the arteries and the most common cause is CHD. It is more common in elderly people and four times more common in men than in women before the menopause. In young men it is the most common cause of death after accidents.

Why is CHD so common in the UK? No one knows for sure, but diet, smoking, lack of exercise and social deprivation seem likely culprits. Of course these problems

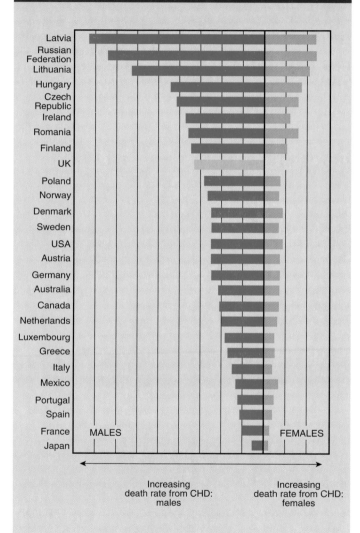

COMPARATIVE DEATH RATE FROM CHD BY COUNTRY

Latvia
Russian Federation
Lithuania
Hungary
Czech Republic
Ireland
Romania
Finland
UK
Poland
Norway
Denmark
Sweden
USA
Austria
Germany
Australia
Canada
Netherlands
Luxembourg
Greece
Italy
Mexico
Portugal
Spain
France
Japan

MALES

FEMALES

Increasing death rate from CHD: males

Increasing death rate from CHD: females

Source: British Heart Foundation Statistics Database, 2000.

all occur in other countries too, which is why there is so much focus on the British diet as the most likely cause. We shall be looking at these factors in more detail later.

NEW TREATMENTS FOR CHD

The last 10 years have seen enormous advances in the treatment of CHD. There are new drugs, such as the 'clot-busters' used after a heart attack, better drugs for angina and powerful cholesterol-lowering drugs, to name just a few. And we have come to understand the value of some of the older drugs such as beta-blockers and aspirin. Not only can these help in relieving symptoms such as pain, they can also slow down or even reverse some of the changes seen in the disease.

The biggest advances, however, have been in the use of surgery and angioplasty. Bypass surgery (CABG – often pronounced as 'cabbage'! – which stands for coronary artery bypass graft) can transform the life of an angina sufferer and in some cases also reduces the risk of further heart attacks. Angioplasty – a technique in which tiny balloons are used to stretch narrowed or blocked arteries – can also be very effective, especially now that fine wire stents (or internal supports) are used to keep the arteries open.

This is all good news for anyone who has heart trouble but our priority as a country should be to tackle the underlying reasons why CHD is so common and try to stop so many people getting it in the first place.

KEY POINTS

✓ CHD is one of the the most common causes of death in the UK

✓ There was an epidemic of CHD in the twentieth century, which is now declining in the UK but rising in countries in eastern Europe

✓ New treatments, including bypass surgery, have helped a lot, but prevention remains better than cure

What goes wrong?

HOW YOUR HEART WORKS

The heart is a muscular pump in the chest which is constantly working, pumping blood around your body, day and night, from the cradle to the grave. It contracts and relaxes 100,000 times a day, and therefore needs a good blood supply of its own – which is provided by the coronary arteries.

The basic function of the heart is to pump red blood, which is rich in oxygen and nutrients, through large arteries to the rest of the body. When the oxygen has been extracted by the tissues, veins carry the blood which is now blue back to the heart.

There are two sides to the heart, each of which acts as a separate pump. The two halves are sub-divided into two chambers, four in

all. The upper ones, the atria, act as collecting reservoirs and the lower ones, the ventricles, contract to pump the blood on. The right side of the heart receives blood through veins from all over the body and pumps it through the lungs so it can pick up oxygen, changing from blue to red. The left side then collects blood returning from the lungs and pumps it round the body to the tissues which need oxygen.

In order to reach all the different organs and muscles, blood has to be pumped at high pressure, as you will certainly know if you have ever cut an artery – the blood spurts everywhere! To do this heart muscle is very strong and it never becomes fatigued, unlike the muscles in our legs, for example. Heart muscle does, however, require a very good

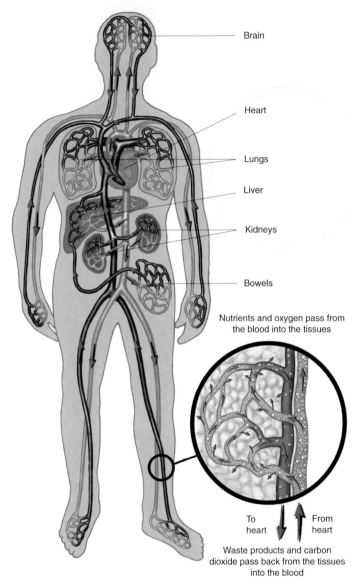

Brain

Heart

Lungs

Liver

Kidneys

Bowels

Nutrients and oxygen pass from
the blood into the tissues

To
heart

From
heart

Waste products and carbon
dioxide pass back from the tissues
into the blood

Diagram showing the heart and circulation with veins (blue) draining the blood back to
the heart where it is pumped to the lungs and back to the rest of the body through the
arteries (red). **Inset:** diagram of the capillary network in tissues such as skin or muscle,
with oxygen and other nutrients passing through the capillary walls to the cells.

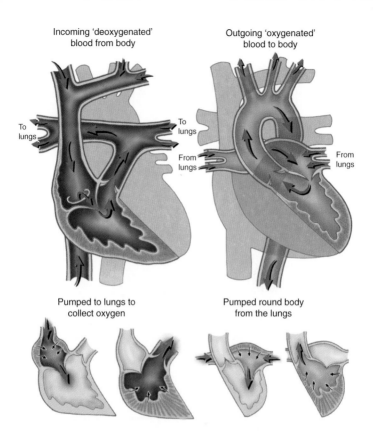

Incoming 'deoxygenated' blood from body

Outgoing 'oxygenated' blood to body

To lungs

To lungs

From lungs

From lungs

Pumped to lungs to collect oxygen

Pumped round body from the lungs

The heart receives blue 'deoxygenated' blood and pumps it through the lungs and then back out, red 'reoxygenated', into the body.

blood supply and this is provided by the coronary arteries and their branches.

THE CORONARY ARTERIES

The coronary arteries come off the aorta – the main blood vessel from the heart – just as it leaves the pumping chamber, the left ventricle, so they are the first arteries to receive blood high in oxygen. The

two arteries, the right and the left, are relatively small (3–4 mm in diameter). They pass over the surface of the heart, meeting each other at the back almost forming a circle. When this pattern of blood vessels was first seen by the ancients, they thought it looked like a crown and so they used the Latin name we have today – the coronary arteries.

As these arteries are so

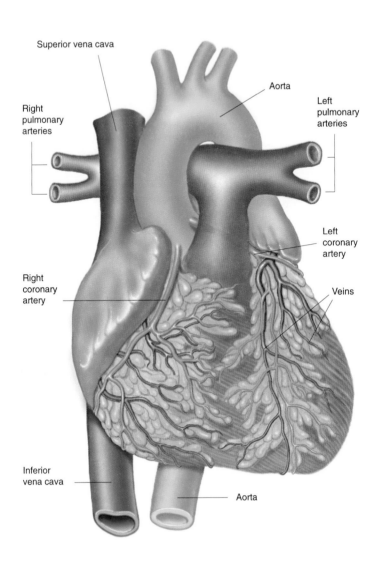

Superior vena cava

Aorta

Right pulmonary arteries

Left pulmonary arteries

Left coronary artery

Right coronary artery

Veins

Inferior vena cava

Aorta

External view of the heart.

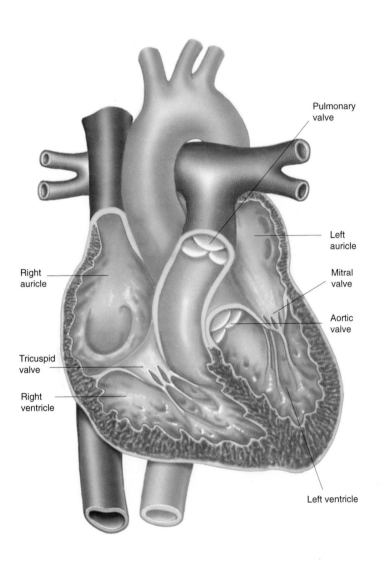

Pulmonary
valve

Left
auricle

Mitral
valve

Aortic
valve

Right
auricle

Tricuspid
valve

Right
ventricle

Left ventricle

Internal view of the heart.

important, doctors are familiar with all their branches and the variations that can arise from one person to another. The left coronary artery has two main branches, called the anterior descending and the circumflex, which in turn have other branches of their own. It supplies most of the left ventricle which is the more muscular of the two ventricles because it has to pump blood around the whole of the body. The right coronary artery is usually smaller and supplies the underside of the heart and the right ventricle, the chamber that pumps blood to the lungs.

The coronary arteries are similar in structure to all other arteries, but are different in one way – blood can only flow through these vessels into the heart muscle between beats as it relaxes. While the heart muscle is contracting, the pressure is too great to allow any blood to pass through the heart muscle itself. This means that the heart requires a very efficient network of fine blood vessels within the heart muscle.

In CHD, the coronary arteries become narrowed (rather like a water pipe becomes 'furred up' in a hard water area), and the heart muscle becomes starved of the blood and oxygen it needs. At rest this may not matter, but if the heart

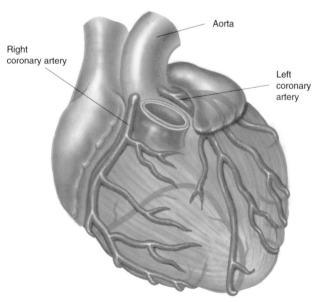

Diagram of the heart showing the left and right coronary arteries arising from the aorta and branching over the surface of the heart.

tries to work harder than normal – for example, if you walk up stairs – the coronary arteries may not be able to keep up with the demand for oxygen, and you get a pain in your chest (see Angina on page 31). If you rest for a while, the pain will usually go away. If a coronary artery becomes completely blocked by a blood clot, the area of the heart muscle it serves will die (see Heart attack on page 18).

Atheroma

Hardening of the arteries, atheroma and atherosclerosis are all the same thing. When you are born, your blood vessels are flexible and elastic and the blood can flow through them with ease. Early in adult life, however, fat deposits can start to form on the walls of the arteries. They gradually build up, forming lumps which protrude into the middle of the artery, and so reduce the blood flow.

The extent of these changes and the rate at which they occur are affected by the level of fat (technically called lipid) in the blood, especially one called low-density lipoprotein cholesterol, or LDL for short (see page 67). People who have high blood levels of LDL cholesterol are more likely to develop severe atheroma, but some changes may be present in all of us by the time we reach middle age.

As the patches of atheroma (or plaques) grow, they thicken and weaken the wall of the artery and progressively reduce the amount of

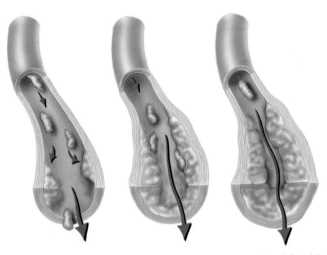

Diagram of blood cells flowing down diseased coronary arteries (seen from left to right with increasing fat deposits obstructing flow).

blood which can flow through it. This process can affect any organ, so that atheroma of the arteries to the brain can lead to a stroke, to the limb, gangrene and, to the heart, a heart attack.

The process of hardening of the arteries is curiously patchy throughout the body, and particularly so in the coronary arteries. The narrowing can just affect one coronary artery or part of one, or it can affect the artery throughout its length, and this may be important in deciding what treatment would suit you best.

In CHD, doctors often talk of one-, two- or three-vessel disease; this refers to whether the three main branches are affected, that is to say, the two main branches of the left coronary artery and the right coronary artery. In general, one- or two-vessel disease may be treated with medicines or angioplasty, whereas three-vessel disease, which affects all the major coronary arteries, usually requires bypass surgery.

Thrombosis

Thrombosis is the medical term for a clot, the natural process that comes into play to stop us bleeding when we injure ourselves. To stop the blood clotting at the wrong time, we also all have chemicals circulating in our blood which are natural anticoagulants or blood thinners. When a blood vessel is damaged, a whole series of chemicals is released close by, activating the blood and causing it to clot. In the case of coronary disease, a clot forms, not because of an outside injury, but as a result of damage to the lining of the artery caused by the fat that has built up in its wall.

Normally, the lining of our arteries is smooth and does not provide any focus on which a clot can form. When atheroma develops the lining is no longer smooth and, where there are breaks in the surface, small cells from the blood called platelets stick to these breaks and help to seal them. Providing the breaks are small, no harm results, but where the artery is critically narrowed even a small clot can have an important effect on blood flow. We now know that such a process is the cause of sudden deterioration in angina – so-called unstable angina (see page 31).

In a heart attack a rather different process is probably responsible. The fatty deposit in the artery does not just contain fat but is also surrounded by scar tissue caused by the cholesterol itself. This forms a fibrous cap over the top of the deposit which is much more rigid than the rest of the artery. Any sudden stress can cause this cap to split, creating a wider area of damage to the wall of the artery.

This results in a much larger clot forming, one that usually blocks the artery altogether. Blood cannot then reach the heart muscle beyond this clot and so that section of muscle dies.

Thrombosis, then, is one of the central problems in coronary heart disease. It is the cause of most cases of sudden deterioration in angina and of most heart attacks. As we shall see, the newer and highly

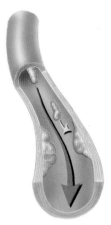

Fat deposits form on the walls of the artery

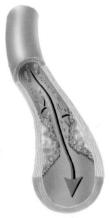

Scar tissue forms a fibrous cap over the fat deposits

The cap is rigid and splits creating a wider area of damage

A large clot forms to seal the damaged area; this blocks the artery

Coronary thrombosis.

effective treatments for coronary heart disease work by removing these clots and preventing their recurrence. We have complex and expensive drugs which can dissolve a clot in a heart attack, and simple, equally effective drugs such as aspirin which can prevent a clot forming in the first place.

We are trying to find out what factors make some people more likely to form blood clots than others. An increased tendency to clot may be one of the as yet undiscovered reasons why in the UK we are more susceptible to coronary heart disease.

THE HEART ATTACK

A heart attack is the final result when the diseased coronary artery becomes completely blocked by a clot, or thrombus. The heart muscle, or myocardium, beyond the clot is suddenly starved of blood and oxygen, and becomes painful, a pain that becomes more intense as the minutes pass. Unless the clot disperses by itself, which doesn't often happen, this area of heart muscle dies within 5 to 10 minutes, resulting in a fully blown heart attack, or myocardial infarction (MI) to give it its technical name.

The actual size of the heart attack and the amount of damaged muscle depends on a number of factors. The first is the size of the artery: the bigger the artery that is

blocked the bigger the area of damage. The second is that the area of damage is generally greater when other coronary arteries are also diseased. Finally, the size of the heart attack depends on whether the area of muscle has developed any collateral blood supply (see page 20). If other collateral arteries have developed to supply the threatened area, the resultant damage is much less. Regular exercise is a good stimulus to the formation of collateral vessels, which is one reason why it forms such an important part of the treatment programmes of people with CHD.

The immediate effect of the damage to the muscle, apart from pain, is that the heart no longer pumps as effectively as before, and the blood pressure may fall, leading to faintness and sweating or nausea. The other major problem in the early stages is that the injury to the muscle causes irregularities of heart rhythm, or cardiac arrhythmias. These irregularities can be life-threatening and lead to a so-called cardiac arrest. As a result of the dangers of these arrhythmias, it is vital that the heart is monitored closely in the first 48 hours or so, and this is usually carried out in hospitals in cardiac care units (CCUs for short). Fortunately, such complications are rare after the first two to three days, and that is when most people can go to the main ward to recover before going home.

After a heart attack, the body begins to repair the damage straight away. Cells remove the dead or damaged muscle and fibrous or scar tissue is formed, a process which takes about six to eight weeks. The scar itself is strong, but unfortunately the heart muscle that has been lost cannot be replaced and some weakening of the heart is inevitable. For most people with a small heart attack this makes very little difference to the overall performance of the heart as a pump. If a larger area of muscle is damaged, however, the heart becomes enlarged, and can no longer pump effectively, a condition we call heart failure.

THE END RESULT

Heart failure can be caused by many diseases affecting the heart, especially high blood pressure, but, in this country, CHD is probably the most common cause. When the heart stops pumping properly, the lungs become congested with blood, leading to breathlessness. Congestion of the rest of the body also leads to fluid retention, which makes the ankles and legs swell. For many years the mainstay of treatment has been the drugs called diuretics or 'water tablets', which get rid of the excess fluid in the body and lungs. Now, however, we have a new class of drug called the ACE (angiotensin-converting enzyme) inhibitors which are even more effective, particularly in reducing the breathlessness.

The other result of the scarring of heart muscle is that it can interfere with the electrical processes responsible for maintaining the normal heart rhythm, and so lead to irregularities, or cardiac arrhythmias. The most common of these is called atrial fibrillation, which is usually treated with digoxin, an old drug derived from the foxglove. Other irregularities can be treated with drugs such as beta-blockers – one of the most useful drugs in CHD – and newer drugs are also now available. See the Family Doctor book *Understanding Heart Failure*.

WHAT HAPPENS WITH TIME

Coronary heart disease is a gradual and unpredictable condition. The fatty deposits in the arteries may build up very slowly over the course of 20 or 30 years. For most of this time there are no symptoms and angina only becomes a problem when one or more of the coronary arteries narrow by more than 70 per cent and blood flow to that part of the heart muscle becomes affected.

As the process is so slow the heart can find ways of overcoming the changes by developing new blood vessels called collaterals. The coronary arteries in effect form a network of blood vessels around the heart and, when one is narrowed, one of the other branches expands to help the area of heart muscle affected.

Although the build-up of coronary atheroma is slow, a clot can occur at any time. People who experience only occasional angina may get a sudden worsening of their condition – unstable angina – or develop a heart attack. Fortunately this doesn't happen very often; only about five per cent of people with angina per year experience such a deterioration.

What is much more worrying is the fact that a heart attack can occur 'out of the blue' in someone who has never been aware that he or she has a heart condition at all. This can happen because quite a small fatty deposit, one that causes no real problem in terms of blood flow, can suddenly split and a clot can block off the artery.

We are now beginning to understand this process rather better and there are a number of drugs which seem able to stop it happening.

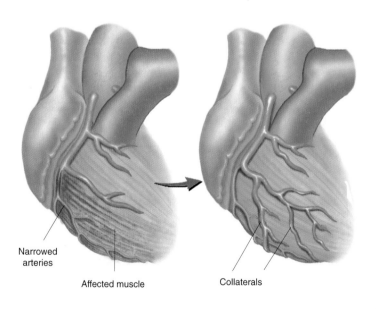

Narrowed arteries

Affected muscle

Collaterals

The heart attack: a blocked artery with damaged heart muscle beyond. Some collateral blood vessels can already be seen supplying the damaged area.

Arthur, aged 64

Three months ago, Arthur found he was getting a pain in his chest whenever he walked up stairs or when he walked up the hill to his home, especially on cold days. His GP told Arthur he had angina and started him on treatment with a regular anti-anginal medicine called atenolol – Arthur now feels well again and has no symptoms.

John, aged 52

John was a keen athlete and ran marathons. His father died of a heart attack (MI) when he was 64. John had been feeling quite well, but he collapsed with chest pain and died suddenly during a 10-mile run. A postmortem examination revealed that the cause of death was a heart attack.

KEY POINTS

✓ To function as a pump, the heart muscle is critically dependent on the coronary arteries for a good blood supply

✓ In CHD, the coronary arteries become narrowed by fatty deposits or atheroma

✓ Narrowing of the coronary arteries can starve the heart muscle of oxygen and this results in the pain of angina

✓ A heart attack results when a diseased coronary artery is blocked completely by a clot, and the heart muscle beyond can die

✓ After a heart attack the damaged muscle heals by forming a scar; providing it is not too big complete recovery can be expected

Causes of CHD – why me?

UNDERSTANDING RISK FACTORS

There does not seem to be one single cause for coronary heart disease, or at least we have not yet found one. Medical research has, however, shown that a whole range of things can make you more likely to develop CHD and these have been called risk factors. Just as a tall person is more likely to hit his head on a door frame than a small one, so people with one or more risk factors are more likely to have a heart attack than those without any. Not every tall person hits his head on a door and not every person with risk factors gets a heart attack, but the likelihood is greater.

The risk factors for CHD are divided into those we can do something about – modifiable – and those we cannot – non-modifiable (see table on page 23). The risk of

you or me developing CHD becomes greater the more risk factors we have, and these risks multiply together. Not all risk factors are equal either. Some, such as smoking, can have a much greater effect on your chances of developing CHD. So, for example, a smoker with a high cholesterol level and high blood pressure has a much higher risk than if he or she had any of these factors by themselves.

However, a high cholesterol level by itself in someone who has no other risk factors means that the risk is increased to only slightly above average. This may well be nothing much to worry about; your doctor will be able to give you individual advice on this.

Age and gender

Heart disease, like many other diseases, becomes more common

RISK FACTORS FOR HEART DISEASE

Modifiable	Non-modifiable
Smoking	Genetic factors, e.g. an inherited
Raised cholesterol	high cholesterol level
High blood pressure	Gender – more men than women
Diabetes	get CHD
Obesity	Age
Stress	
Lack of exercise	

the older we get. In the UK at present, half the heart attacks occur in people over the age of 65, and the numbers are rising as the average age of the population increases.

The striking thing about CHD is that, below the age of 55, it is a much more common disease among men than women. This is because, before the menopause (the change of life when women stop menstruating), women very rarely have heart attacks. After the menopause, CHD becomes more common so that the rate among women gradually catches up with men, and over the age of 75 the numbers are about equal.

The exact reason why women are protected from CHD before the menopause is not known for sure but it does seem likely that this is related to hormones that disappear once menstruation stops. Many women are now taking HRT for

other reasons and this may help prevent a heart attack. However, most doctors would not now prescribe HRT purely to prevent heart disease.

Family history

Doctors talk about a positive family history when one or more close relatives (parents, brothers, sisters or children) have had CHD. If your father had a heart attack below the age of 60 or your mother below the age of 65, this increases your own risk of CHD. Of course, if your parents lived to old age when heart attacks are common, this is not so important.

The same also applies to brothers and sisters, although, in very large families, the fact that one member may have a heart attack could be just the result of chance.

How is it that CHD runs in families? Part of the explanation is the genes we inherit from our parents that may make us more liable to have high cholesterol or develop high blood pressure or diabetes. Part of it is also the result of families living similar lifestyles – they all eat the same food and, if parents smoke, often their children do too.

If heart disease does appear to run in your family it is very useful to have check-ups from time to time with your doctor, to make sure that you have not developed high cholesterol, high blood pressure or other problems which could be treated to reduce your risk.

Diet and cholesterol

As we have already seen, atheroma is the major cause of coronary artery disease. Deposits of fat and, especially, of cholesterol, known as plaques, form in the walls of the arteries. This makes them narrower and so reduces blood flow. When the plaques split, a clot forms on the damaged area, stopping the blood reaching a part of the heart muscle. This is what happens in a heart attack. This whole process is more likely to happen (and to cause more damage if it does) in a person who has a high level of cholesterol in the blood.

Your genetic make-up is partly responsible for determining your cholesterol level. Some families carry genes for raised levels of various kinds of blood fats. This condition is called familial hyperlipidaemia or FH for short. However, diet also plays an important part in

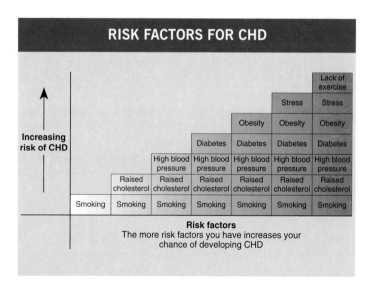

RISK FACTORS FOR CHD

						Lack of exercise
					Stress	Stress
				Obesity	Obesity	Obesity
			Diabetes	Diabetes	Diabetes	Diabetes
		High blood pressure	High blood pressure	High blood pressure	High blood pressure	High blood pressure
	Raised cholesterol	Raised cholesterol	Raised cholesterol	Raised cholesterol	Raised cholesterol	Raised cholesterol
Smoking	Smoking	Smoking	Smoking	Smoking	Smoking	Smoking

Increasing risk of CHD ↑

Risk factors
The more risk factors you have increases your chance of developing CHD

determining cholesterol levels. The more fats – particularly animal and dairy fat – you eat, the higher your cholesterol will be and the higher your risk of CHD (see diagram on page 26). So it really is worth reducing the animal fat content in your diet (for more on this, see pages 69–72).

Smoking

Cigarette smoking is strongly linked to the risk of CHD. Chemicals in cigarette smoke are absorbed into your bloodstream from the lungs and circulate around the body, affecting every cell. These chemicals make the blood vessels narrow temporarily. They also cause blood cells called platelets to become stickier, so increasing the chance of a clot forming.

Pipe and cigar smokers do not have the high risk of cigarette smokers but are still more likely to get CHD than non-smokers. The amount you smoke also matters; the risk rises stepwise between light (fewer than 10 cigarettes per day), moderate (10–20 cigarettes per day) and heavy smokers (more than 20 cigarettes per day).

The reason why doctors place such stress on stopping smoking is that it is the one risk factor that you can control yourself. What's more, you start to reap the benefit from the moment you stop. Although

THE FRAMINGHAM STUDY

One of the first studies that linked high cholesterol with CHD was carried out after World War II in a small town near Boston, USA called Framingham. All the residents were examined at yearly intervals to see whether or not they had developed CHD. A strong link with raised cholesterol was found early on – the higher the blood cholesterol, the higher the risk of developing a heart attack. The Framingham study also showed the importance of the other risk factors such as smoking, high blood pressure and diabetes, and these risk factors have been confirmed over a follow-up period of nearly 40 years since the study first started. The study is still continuing.

your risk of CHD may never be quite as low as that of a non-smoker, it certainly comes close to it a year or two after stopping.

Stress

Many people who have had a heart attack point to some personal stress as a cause, but it has been surprisingly difficult to prove this link scientifically. There are well-recognised trigger factors, such as sudden unexpected exercise and extreme emotional experiences, which can bring on a heart attack, but this is a fairly rare occurrence. And at times of great civil and military stress, such as in World War II, the number of heart attacks in the civilian population actually fell.

We also often think of certain personality types as having a higher risk of heart disease. Modern technology has brought with it the ability to do things in minutes which even a generation ago might have taken days. The pressure to take on more than you can manage, to set unrealistic goals, has created the idea of the type A personality. This restless individual (usually male) finds it difficult to relax, becomes increasingly tied up in work at the expense of personal relationships and is prone in the end to 'burn-out'; he is said to have double the risk of CHD compared with the 'laid-back' type B personality.

This theory linking CHD and the stressful personality was once very fashionable, and a lot of effort was devoted to trying to persuade people who had worked hard all their lives that they must relax. Modern research has failed to confirm these earlier findings and,

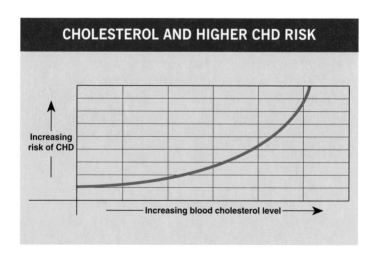

CHOLESTEROL AND HIGHER CHD RISK

Increasing risk of CHD

Increasing blood cholesterol level →

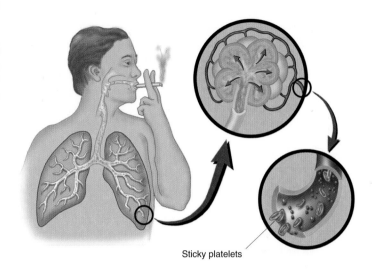

Smoking makes blood platelets 'stickier', so increasing the likelihood of blood clots forming in the circulation.

although a major illness of any kind is a time to take stock of priorities in life, attempts to make major changes in behaviour are probably of little benefit.

Other diseases linked to CHD

Two common and important diseases are associated with a higher than average risk of CHD: high blood pressure (BP) and diabetes.

• **High blood pressure:** The term blood pressure actually means the pressure in the arteries taking blood from the heart to the rest of the body. High blood pressure causes stresses on the heart and circulation

and most people are aware that it causes strokes. However, in the UK high BP is responsible for more heart attacks than strokes, probably because of the high cholesterol levels present in this country. Treatment of high blood pressure will reduce the risk of both heart attack and stroke.

Blood pressure is usually measured in the upper arm. With each beat of the heart, the blood pressure rises to a high point (systolic pressure) then falls to a low point between beats (diastolic pressure). This pressure is measured in millimetres of mercury (mmHg). An average healthy person's blood pressure at rest is around 120/70, said as 120 over 70. A resting pressure of 140/90 is borderline, whereas 150/100 is definitely raised.

High blood pressure (or hypertension) is found right across the world and is particularly common in Afro-Caribbean countries and black Americans. It is also, however, very common in the UK, with perhaps 25 per cent of the population over the age of 50 having high blood pressure readings.

The cause of high blood pressure is not known in most people. It does run in families and is seen in people with kidney disease. Unfortunately, in most cases high blood pressure gives rise to no symptoms, and it is for this reason that it is sensible to have your blood pressure checked from time to time in case it is high and you don't know it.

The high pressure in the arteries damages the lining and accelerates the development of atheroma. The heart also has to work harder to pump blood under high pressure, but it must do so without an adequate supply of oxygen. This increases the person's chances of developing angina or having a heart attack. High blood pressure also increases the risk of a stroke because of the damage it causes to blood vessels in the brain. See the Family Doctor book *Understanding Blood Pressure.*

• **Diabetes:** This is a common condition which affects roughly three in 100 people in the UK. It is caused by a deficiency of, or a resistance to, the hormone insulin, which is essential to control the movement of glucose into cells around the body via the bloodstream.

Diabetes can affect people of any age, including children, and the younger you are when you get diabetes, the more likely you are to need insulin injections to control it. Many people, however, get diabetes in middle or old age. When this happens, there are few symptoms and the condition can be controlled by diet and tablets. The aim of treatment is to keep the level of glucose in the blood as close as possible to normal. Nevertheless, despite treatment, diabetes can increase the risk of many circulatory disorders including CHD. For women this is particularly important because it seems to counteract the protective effect of female hormones and almost as many women as men with diabetes develop CHD.

Good control of diabetes, with diet, tablets or insulin, makes heart and circulatory problems less common. Poor control can often result in very abnormal blood fats, including cholesterol, and people with diabetes may need to take additional drugs to control this.

See the Family Doctor book *Understanding Diabetes*.

FINALLY ...

But it's not all bad news. There are lifestyle factors such as alcohol which can reduce the risk of developing CHD and we will be looking at those on page 73.

People often feel guilty about having heart disease as if it is somehow their fault.

That isn't fair; the fact is simply that we know so much more about the factors that lead to CHD than we do about almost any other important disease.

KEY POINTS

✓ CHD is much more common in men than in women, and in the old than in the young

✓ Important risk factors for CHD are smoking, raised blood cholesterol, high blood pressure and diabetes

✓ Stopping smoking and reducing cholesterol and blood pressure levels cut the risk of CHD

Recognising the symptoms

Although most people with CHD have the same underlying problem, namely narrowing of the coronary arteries, they don't all get the same symptoms. Some develop angina, others may have a heart attack. A smaller proportion of people may develop heart failure without having any previous warning symptoms. We don't know the reasons why it affects people in different ways.

CHEST PAIN

Not all chest pain is caused by CHD! No one would jump to the conclusion that they had heart disease after falling and bruising their ribs, for example, and most of us have had experience of indigestion which can sometimes be painful too.

You might think that it would be easy to distinguish chest pain caused by heart disease from any

HOW TO RECOGNISE HEART PAIN

- A dull pain which does not feel worse when you breathe in
- Usually in the middle of the chest but may spread into the left side, into both arms or up into the neck or jaw
- Could be described as: heavy, burning, vice-like or like a weight on the chest

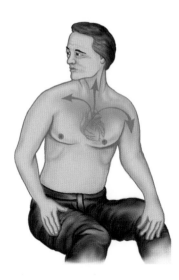

Pain from the heart is usually felt beneath the breast bone in the centre of the chest, but may spread into either arm (even to the finger tips) and to the jaw or back.

it can come on after quite mild exertion, such as getting dressed. It's usually worse in the cold weather and if you exercise after a meal – taking the dog for a walk after breakfast, for example.

• **Unstable angina:** In general, angina is fairly predictable, but, if the coronary artery narrows still further or a clot forms on its surface, then the disease can enter a new phase – unstable angina. You may suddenly find that you can only walk a short distance before developing pain, or you may develop pain doing light work around the house or even going upstairs to bed. Sometimes you may be woken from sleep by an attack of angina. A change in the pattern of pain is an important development and should be reported to your doctor. Unstable angina can lead to a heart attack and it is important to take steps to prevent this.

other kind, but in fact it can be difficult, even for the most experienced doctor.

• **Angina:** Angina pectoris is simply the Latin for pain in the chest, and it is brought on by exercise, going away when you rest. In CHD, the pain comes from the muscle fibres in the heart, which don't have enough oxygen for the work they are doing.

Angina usually lasts for about two or three minutes and no more than 10. It may only come on when you walk uphill, into a strong wind or when you're climbing stairs, but

• **Heart attack:** The pain is the same as angina, but instead of easing off when you rest, it gets worse. People who've experienced it often say it's the worst pain they've ever felt in their lives. Someone who is having a heart attack may look grey and sweaty, and feel cold to the touch. They often feel sick and may vomit. Some people who have heart attacks have

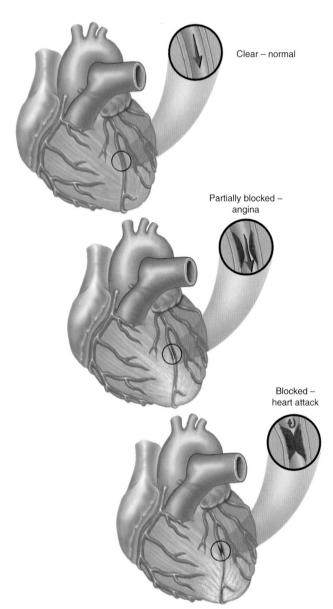

Clear – normal

Partially blocked – angina

Blocked – heart attack

Diagram of the heart showing, from top to bottom: normal heart with clear coronary arteries; narrowed coronary artery giving angina; blocked coronary artery leading to a heart attack.

never had any symptoms of heart disease – it just comes out of the blue. Most, however, will have had some pain off and on for weeks or months before as the blood vessels gradually narrowed.

The difference between angina and a heart attack is that, whereas angina leaves the heart muscle short of oxygen but basically undamaged, in a heart attack a part of the heart muscle actually dies as a result of oxygen shortage.

In about 20 per cent of cases, the symptoms of a heart attack may be mild and are often mistaken for indigestion. This is particularly true of elderly people and those with diabetes, perhaps because the pain fibres to the heart are not as sensitive in these two groups of people.

OTHER CAUSES OF CHEST PAIN

We all experience pains in the chest from time to time as we do in other parts of our body. The most likely causes are the following.

Indigestion or 'heartburn'

The gullet (or oesophagus), which leads from the mouth to the stomach, lies just behind the heart and has the same nerve supply, so it is not surprising that pain from the gullet – heartburn – may feel much like pain from the heart. Heartburn can occur at any time but is usually related to food, starting half an hour or so after meals or when the stomach is empty.

Heartburn can also occur at night when you lie flat because some of the acid from the stomach spills back into the gullet and irritates it. Eating more food or drinking milk or antacids eases heartburn, and hot fluids and alcohol make it worse.

Indigestion is not, however, brought on by exercise and if you feel a pain in your chest when you walk – even if it makes you belch – it is much more likely to be from your heart than from your stomach. See your doctor!

Pleurisy

Chest infections such as pneumonia can give rise to quite bad chest pain called pleurisy. The pain is usually sharp, only on one side of the chest and is worse when you cough or take a deep breath. This is quite different from the dull constant pain from the heart which spreads right across the chest.

Muscle pain

Along the back and between the ribs there are muscles that play an important part in breathing and, like all muscles, they can be subject to rheumatic pain. This pain is usually confined to a fairly small area of the chest, either at the front or at the back. It is worse when sitting or

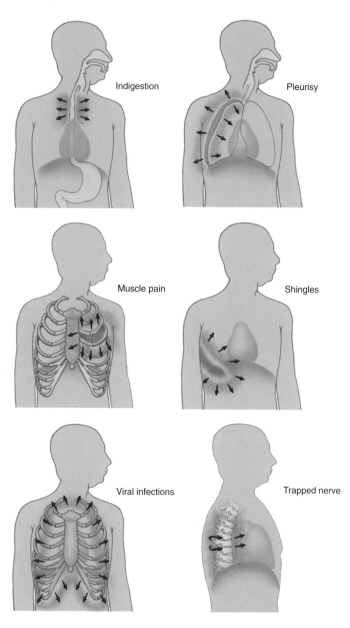

Indigestion

Pleurisy

Muscle pain

Shingles

Viral infections

Trapped nerve

Chest pain can have many causes not related to the heart.

lying in certain positions or when you turn round. It can last from a few hours to a few days and then may disappear before returning again a few weeks later.

There are other possible causes of chest pain, although they are less common.

• **Shingles:** This infection can cause severe pain around the chest for two or three days before the tell-tale blistering rash appears in the painful area.

• **Viral infections:** Some cold or 'flu-like viruses can affect the cartilage which attaches the ribs to the breastbone. When this happens, the chest will feel tender when you press it and the pain is quite different from heart pain.

• **Trapped nerve:** Sometimes, pressure on a nerve in the back or neck can cause pain that spreads down the arm or around the chest. This can be caused by damage to a disc or by arthritis in the spine. Another relatively common cause, particularly in older women, is collapse of a bone in the spine. This is usually the result of a condition called osteoporosis in which the bones become thin and fragile.

PALPITATIONS

Palpitations – when the heart beats irregularly or misses a beat – are very common in healthy people. They are usually brought on by stress, smoking or drinking too much coffee and tea. A few people may also have an electrical 'short circuit' in the heart which gives rise to a very rapid heart beat, but this is uncommon.

People with CHD can also develop problems with heart rhythm but this is most likely after a heart attack and your doctor will then give special drugs to try and control this. If your palpitations are associated with faintness, breath-lessness or chest pain, you should tell your doctor as soon as possible.

BREATHLESSNESS AND SWOLLEN ANKLES

There are many possible reasons for breathlessness, of which the most common are chronic bronchitis, emphysema and asthma. Heart failure also causes breathlessness and can affect someone who has had a heart attack (see page 19). If the heart isn't pumping properly, fluid tends to build up in the tissues and lungs, and the result is breathlessness.

You may then find it difficult to lie flat in bed or wake up in the night with problems getting your breath. You may also develop a cough with a little frothy or blood-stained sputum.

When fluid builds up elsewhere in the body, you may find that your ankles swell or that you get pain in the stomach because your liver and gut are swollen. When you are known to have a heart condition, increasing breathlessness or a cough that won't go away may be important. There are now good drugs for treating heart failure and the sooner you seek help the better.

KEY POINTS

✓ When the heart muscle is short of oxygen, the result is chest pain – either angina or a heart attack

✓ Severe chest pain is a heart attack until proved otherwise

✓ Angina pain usually comes on when you exercise or are under stress

✓ Indigestion is not usually brought on by exercise; if in doubt seek advice

Tests for CHD

There are many possible causes of chest pain and the most important clue as to whether this pain is from the heart lies in what type of pain it is and when it comes on (see pages 30–5).

Doctors are usually able to distinguish between the different types of pain in the chest. It may become very clear, simply from what you tell the doctor, that the pain is coming from your heart or that there is nothing to worry about.

The pain from a heart attack or from angina is often unmistakable. However, there are other times when the diagnosis is less clear-cut and the doctor then has to make a decision based upon how likely it is that you might have CHD. In a young woman, chest pain is much more likely to be indigestion than angina whereas, in a middle-aged man who smokes and has high blood pressure, it is more likely to be angina than indigestion.

Experience counts, but unfortunately no doctor is infallible, and many doctors have not even been able to diagnose their own heart attack! But, because CHD is so common in the UK, most doctors will arrange further tests if there is any doubt about the diagnosis.

HEART TRACING

Resting ECG

The most common test for heart conditions is the electrocardiograph or ECG for short (in America it is called the EKG, as it is based on the German word). It is a simple, painless test that takes about 10 minutes and can be done by your GP or practice nurse.

Every time the heart beats, it causes natural electrical changes which can be picked up by electrodes placed at various points around the body. These electrodes, covered in a sticky gel to ensure a good contact, are usually put on the ankles, wrists and across the chest.

The tracing records the heart rate and rhythm and whether the muscle is conducting electricity normally. Damaged muscle or muscle that is short of oxygen will result in a different appearance.

The resultant tracing gives the doctor a lot of information about the heart, but, like most tests, the ECG is not infallible. If you have angina, your heart trace may still be normal if it is recorded at rest when free of pain. In this case, you may need an exercise ECG.

Exercise ECG

Any form of exercise can be used to provoke angina. In the UK, we generally use a treadmill test, but in Europe they often use a bicycle. ECG electrodes are attached just as for the resting ECG, but the wires are attached carefully to the chest so that they don't come loose while you are walking. The treadmill usually starts at a slow pace on the flat and then increases every two or three minutes to a faster speed on an increasing slope so that you are effectively walking uphill. The test is stopped if you develop pain, if there are major ECG changes or, of

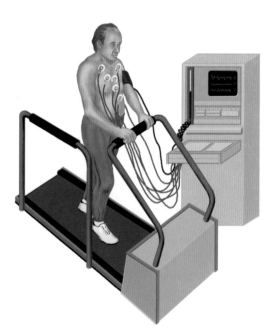

Exercise ECG using a treadmill.

course, if you become tired or too breathless.

The useful thing about the exercise ECG is that it gives two bits of information to the doctor. The first is that, if the test produces pain and ECG changes, it confirms the diagnosis of angina. The second and just as important is that, if you manage to walk a fair distance before the pain comes on, it tells the doctor that the angina is mild and further tests may not be necessary.

The test is done as a hospital out-patient and takes about 40 minutes.

RADIOACTIVE ISOTOPE TESTS

These tests make use of chemicals, or isotopes, which give out very small amounts of radioactivity that can be picked up by a special camera. Different tissues around the body take up different isotopes. For the heart various isotopes are used, the most common being thallium and technetium. Both these are taken up by heart muscle with a normal blood supply but would not be taken up by muscle which has a poor blood supply. So where there is a narrowing or blockage of a coronary artery, that area of heart muscle will not be seen as well as the rest of the heart.

Isotopes are radioactive, but the amount of radioactivity given in these tests is small and equivalent to most standard X-ray procedures.

The isotope breaks down quickly in the body and some of it is passed in the urine, but it does not pose any danger to you or anybody else.

The isotope scan is carried out in two stages, once when the heart is stressed and once again when it is at rest, and the two images are compared. The stress pictures are usually taken after a treadmill test but, for those who can't exercise, the heart can be stimulated by drugs, the two most common being an injection of dipyridamole or dobutamine. At the end of the exercise test or after giving the drug, an injection of isotope is given and you then lie under the camera for 10 or 15 minutes while the pictures are taken.

Sometimes, the isotope scan is better at picking up abnormalities than the exercise ECG, and it is useful after bypass surgery when the arterial supply to the heart can become quite complicated. It is also the only way to study the heart in people who can't manage the treadmill or bicycle, for example, because of arthritis or bad lung disease.

STRESS ECHOCARDIOGRAPHY

This is a technique that is similar in principle to the isotope test, except that radioactivity is not involved. Echocardiography is the name given to the scanner which uses sound

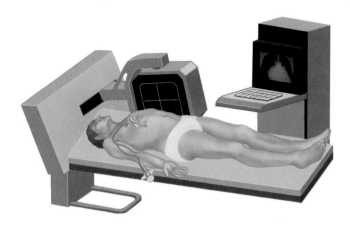

Isotope study of the heart. The camera passes over the body to pick up the radiation from the isotope that has been injected.

beams to take pictures of the heart and is just the same as the ultrasound scanner used to see the baby in a mother's womb.

With this type of scanner, it is possible to see the heart muscle contracting and to pick out any parts that are contracting poorly because the blood supply has been cut off. As in the isotope study, the heart can be stimulated either by exercise or by the injection of drugs

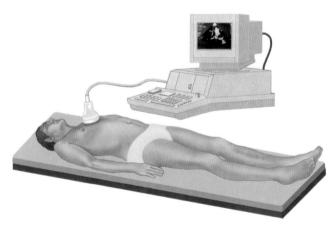

Echocardiography uses sound beams to take pictures.

and the heart is scanned before, during and after the stress. The pictures are then analysed in detail and can give good information as to which arteries may be blocked and how badly.

CORONARY ANGIOGRAPHY

The most direct way of finding out what is wrong with the heart is to undertake special X-rays of the coronary arteries, called angiograms. These are X-rays in which dye that can be seen on an X-ray is injected directly into the coronary arteries. As the heart is moving all the time, the X-rays have to be taken on cine-film or video, so it requires expensive equipment which at one time was only available in a few large teaching hospitals. With modern technology, these facilities are more widely available and most district hospitals can now undertake angiography.

In order to take a picture of these small arteries, the dye needs to be injected directly into them. To do this, a fine tube called a catheter has to be passed to the heart, usually from an artery in the groin, but sometimes from an artery at the wrist or elbow. A little local anaesthetic is injected under the skin to numb it. The catheter is then passed up through the artery towards the heart. You will not be aware of this happening, although when the tube reaches the heart you may have a few palpitations. This is quite normal.

Once the tube is in the coronary artery, dye is injected and pictures taken from various angles. While this is being done, you will be asked to hold your breath for perhaps five or ten seconds. The dye itself may cause a little flushing which passes off quickly.

Coronary angiography is a safe and routine procedure. Serious complications are rare – less than one in 1,000. The most important risk, which fortunately is very rare, is that the investigation can provoke a heart attack. If this should happen, emergency surgery may be needed. Less serious complications are an allergy to the dye or damage to the artery in the groin or at the wrist.

Although coronary angiography is the best way of looking at the coronary arteries, it is not necessary for everyone with angina or CHD. Most doctors will use it only where they think there is a real possibility that you might benefit from heart surgery or angioplasty (see pages 47–53). Coronary angiography is often done as a day case procedure and takes about 40 minutes. You probably won't have to stay in hospital overnight but you will need to lie down for three or four hours afterwards to reduce the risk of any bleeding. The area used for the test will often be bruised and may be a little tender for a few days.

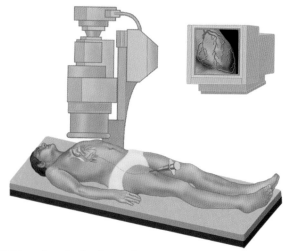

Coronary angiography: the diagram shows the catheter being passed from an artery in the groin to the heart. Dye is injected and pictures are taken by the X-ray camera which moves overhead to different positions.

KEY POINTS

✓ The most common test for heart disease is the ECG, but it is not infallible

✓ If the resting ECG is normal, a treadmill exercise test is a good way to show angina and see how serious it is

✓ For anyone who can't exercise, radioisotope testing or echocardiography may be used instead

✓ Coronary angiography is the best way of identifying which arteries are affected, but is not needed by everyone with CHD

Treating angina

ngina is pain in the chest caused by inadequate amounts of oxygen reaching the heart muscle. It usually comes on after exercise and disappears after you have rested for a few minutes. Unstable angina is when the condition gets rapidly worse so that eventually you are in pain even when resting. It may be a warning of an impending heart attack.

The doctor's aim when treating angina is to increase the amount you can do before pain starts and/or to relieve pain once it has started. Treatment may be with drugs, angioplasty or surgery.

MEDICAL TREATMENTS

Usually drug treatment will be tried first. Drugs work by reducing the amount of oxygen needed by the heart muscle or increasing the blood flow to the heart, or both.

Whatever treatment your doctor starts you on, it is important that you work together as a partnership. You must take your medication as prescribed – in most cases, this is likely to be once or twice a day. You should also make any necessary adjustments to your lifestyle. This might mean giving up smoking, losing weight and taking more exercise. You will find more about this in the section beginning on page 66.

Nitrates

Nitrates in various forms have been used for angina for more than 100 years, and are the most common drugs used to relieve the pain of angina. Glyceryl trinitrate (or GTN for short) is absorbed very quickly through the lining of the mouth and is either taken as a small tablet under the tongue or as a spray. It opens up, or dilates, the coronary arteries and so improves the blood flow to the heart muscle in areas where the coronary arteries are narrowed.

Nitrates also dilate the arteries and veins throughout the body and this can lead to side effects, particularly dizziness and headache. If you do feel dizzy after using GTN sit or lie down for a few minutes when the effect will usually pass off. The headache which often occurs after using GTN is caused by the blood vessels to the brain dilating. It usually comes on within a minute or two of taking the nitrate and disappears quickly if you spit the tablet out.

People often find that the pain from angina starts to ease as the headache comes on. The effect of nitrates is so predictable in CHD that doctors often use this to tell whether your chest pain is really angina. This is fairly reliable but pain from the gullet (oesophagus) can also sometimes be eased by GTN which can be confusing.

Anyone who has angina should always keep their GTN tablets or spray with them wherever they are in case they get an unexpected attack of chest pain. However, if you have opened a bottle of tablets but not used any for a while, do keep an eye on the expiry date – GTN tablets will not work once the bottle has been open for more than six weeks.

As we have seen, GTN works very quickly indeed, so if the pain has not settled within five minutes of taking the medicine, it may be

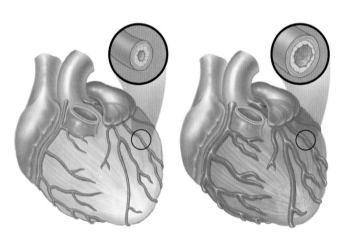

Coronary arteries (diseased) dilating after GTN.

developing into something more serious. Your doctor will probably advise you to wait for five minutes and if there has been no improvement to take another dose.

IF THE CHEST PAIN IS STILL NO BETTER 10 MINUTES AFTER A SECOND DOSE OF GTN, YOU SHOULD SEEK IMMEDIATE MEDICAL HELP.

Nitrates can be swallowed as a tablet but are not absorbed all that well from the stomach, which is why other, more effective ways of taking them have been developed. Some special formulations include a longer-acting tablet which can be left between the gums and the cheek for several hours (called buccal nitrate). There is even a skin patch containing GTN. This is a transparent plaster containing the drug which is absorbed slowly through the skin. It is left on for 18 hours and is usually removed at night. Your doctor may try several different nitrates to find out which suits you best.

Beta-blockers

Beta-blockers are a group of drugs that were discovered 30 years ago and were a major advance in the treatment of angina. They were called beta-blockers because they block the effects of adrenaline on so-called beta receptors in the heart, lungs and blood vessels. Their effect is to slow down the heart beat and reduce the blood pressure, particularly during exercise, so enabling the heart to undertake more work before angina comes on. People with angina usually find that they can walk further than they could before, and have to use their GTN less often. Sometimes, people find that the angina disappears altogether, though it would probably come on if they exercised hard enough.

Unfortunately, beta-blockers do not suit everybody. They cannot be given to people with bronchitis or asthma as they make breathing even more difficult. Other possible side effects include cold hands and feet, aching in the leg muscles when walking, tiredness and, occasionally, impotence. There are, however, more than a dozen different beta-blockers available at present and often people find that one suits them better than another.

Calcium channel blockers

Calcium channel blockers slow down the rate at which calcium can enter body cells, particularly in the heart muscle and blood vessel walls. This group of drugs has been developed over the last 20 years; they act rather like nitrates by dilating the coronary arteries and improving the blood flow to the heart muscle. Like beta-blockers they increase the amount of exercise you can manage before getting angina though they do not slow the heart rate. As they act in a different way, they can be used with beta-blockers or nitrates as

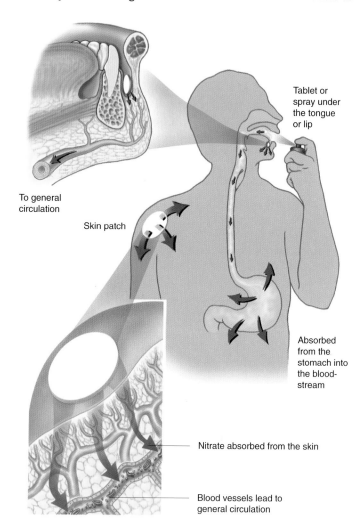

Tablet or spray under the tongue or lip

To general circulation

Skin patch

Absorbed from the stomach into the bloodstream

Nitrate absorbed from the skin

Blood vessels lead to general circulation

Some of the ways in which nitrates can be taken.

well as by themselves. The most common side effects, as with nitrates, are headaches and dizziness. They can also cause swelling of the ankles and constipation.

Aspirin

Aspirin should be taken by everyone with angina, providing it does not upset them. It works by 'thinning' the blood so that it clots less easily. The danger for someone with angina is that a clot will form in any narrowed coronary artery and lead to a heart attack. By reducing the risk of clots forming, aspirin reduces the risk of a heart attack.

The amount of aspirin needed to do this is only 75 milligrams a day – a quarter of an ordinary aspirin tablet or equivalent to the old junior aspirin. At these low doses side effects are rare but there are some people who are allergic to aspirin (especially those with asthma) or who find it gives them indigestion.

Clopidogrel

We now have a new drug, clopidogrel, which acts in a similar manner to aspirin to thin the blood, but it does not cause as much indigestion. New research also shows that it is very useful in unstable angina when used in combination with aspirin. So, if you have recently been in hospital with angina, you may well come out taking both.

Other drugs

Other drugs are being developed all the time for the treatment of angina and your doctor may wish to use one of these in your case, either because others have not worked or because they have had side effects.

Nicorandil is one of these newer drugs and acts a bit like nitrates and calcium channel blockers to dilate the coronary arteries. It does so, however, by a different mechanism and may work when nitrates don't.

In some situations your doctor may also try warfarin, a drug that 'thins' the blood even more than aspirin. This can, like aspirin, reduce the risk of a heart attack and it may also help angina.

ANGIOPLASTY AND SURGERY

By no means everyone with angina will need an operation but, where the symptoms are becoming difficult to control with drugs, the results of surgery can be dramatic. An individual who has had angina for years, for example, can walk without difficulty again and some have even completed marathons! There are now many procedures which can be used to improve blood flow, either by bypassing arteries (coronary artery bypass surgery or CABG) or by stretching them (coronary angioplasty or PCI).

Although both CABG and PCI work well, they are not really a 'cure' in the sense that they do not get rid of the basic problem which is the 'furring' up of the coronary arteries.

You still need to take all the steps necessary to prevent the arteries from deteriorating, either by changes in lifestyle such as stopping smoking, or with drugs such as those to lower cholesterol, and sometimes both (see pages 66–74).

Angioplasty

Angioplasty was first used about 20 years ago and involves stretching narrowed areas of blood vessels to improve blood flow. This is much quicker and easier than CABG but may be less reliable in the long term.

In principle, angioplasty is a technique whereby a long, thin balloon is passed across the narrowed region of a blood vessel, over a very fine guide wire. The balloon is then inflated at high pressure and stretches the artery, often splitting the fatty deposits in its wall. When the balloon is deflated and removed, the artery remains open.

The problem with coronary angioplasty is that, in one in four people, the narrowing may come back within a few weeks or months – either the artery is not stretched far enough in the first place or inflammation sets in. If this happens, a second angioplasty may well be successful. There has, however,

HAVING AN ANGIOPLASTY

The operation is usually done on an overnight basis – you go in in the morning and come home the next day. From your point of view, the procedure is exactly the same as having coronary angiography (see page 41). A deflated balloon is passed with a fine wire into narrowed areas of the blood vessels and then inflated. It is then removed – and you won't have felt any of this happening. Sometimes you may experience some chest pain during the procedure and there is a one to two per cent chance that angioplasty may cause a sudden blockage, necessitating an emergency CABG. Usually, however, you'll be back to normal after a week. Angioplasty can be repeated later, more than once if necessary.

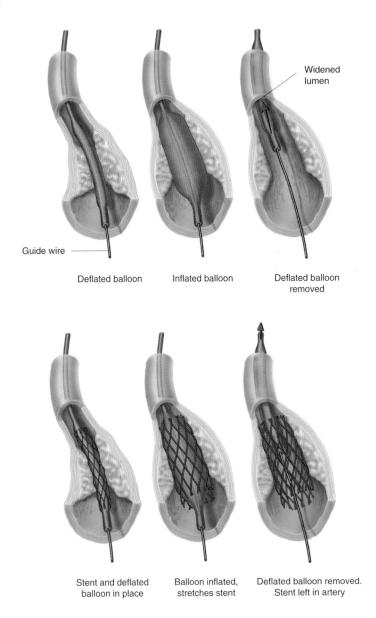

Widened lumen

Guide wire

Deflated balloon

Inflated balloon

Deflated balloon removed

Stent and deflated balloon in place

Balloon inflated, stretches stent

Deflated balloon removed. Stent left in artery

Coronary angioplasty (above), and with stent placement (below).

been a big advance over the last few years with the use of coronary stents.

A stent is a fine wire mesh which is stretched over the balloon and, as the balloon is blown up, it stretches with the artery and remains there to hold it open once the balloon has been removed. Stents have reduced the risks of recurrence substantially, making angioplasty an effective long-term treatment for patients with angina.

Unfortunately, this exciting new technique is not suitable for everybody. It is best for people with one or two areas of narrowing in large arteries, and is really no good for those who have small vessels or narrowing in all three coronary arteries. In these cases bypass surgery may be a better long-term solution.

Bypass surgery

Bypass surgery has been one of the major advances in the treatment of angina. The name derives from the effect of the operation which is to bypass the blockages in the coronary arteries using replacement blood vessels taken from the chest wall or the legs. You may also hear the term 'bypass' used to mean the

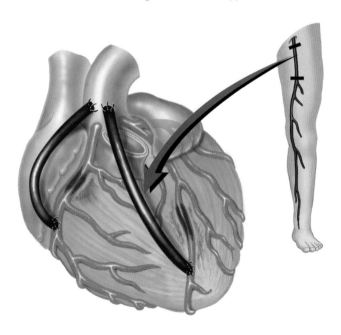

Coronary bypass surgery, showing one vein graft taken from the leg.

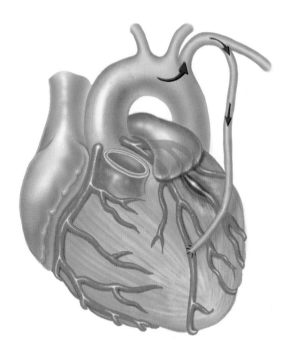

Coronary bypass surgery, showing one graft from the internal mammary artery.

technique carried out by surgeons when they stop the heart and let the heart–lung machine take over the circulation during the operation.

When the operation was first performed surgeons used veins removed from the leg. These were cut into lengths of four to five inches (10 to 13 centimetres) and sewn between the blocked coronary arteries and the aorta (the main artery leading from the heart to the rest of the body).

In the last 10 years techniques have changed and, whenever possible, most surgeons now use small arteries rather than vein grafts. The long-term results of this technique appear to be better than with veins, which were never made to withstand the pressures normally present in the coronary arteries.

The two most commonly used arteries are the internal mammary arteries which run down behind the breast bone. They can be attached to either the left or right coronary artery. More recently surgeons have even used arteries from the stomach or from the arm and both of these may last better than the vein grafts.

Major heart surgery is not without risks and would not be recommended for everyone with angina, particularly if the symptoms were mild. There are, however, some people with mild angina who may need bypass surgery because they have a high risk of a heart attack. This is usually because angiography has shown that all three coronary arteries are affected (see page 16).

A few people still have angina after CABG because it may not be possible to bypass all the blockages. Bypassing all the main arteries will reduce the risk of further heart attacks but some of the arteries may be too small to operate on, so mild angina may still occur, although it can often be controlled with drugs.

Unfortunately the new blood vessels may not last for ever and if they do narrow or block a second operation may be needed. A second bypass can be more risky than the first, but using the new technique with mammary arteries, the long-term results can be just as good or better.

HAVING A CABG

Usually, you will be admitted to hospital for one or two days before your operation for final tests and assessment.

On the day itself, you will go to sleep in the anaesthetic room and wake up in ITU (intensive care), probably still on a ventilator which is doing your breathing for you.

You often have a lot of drips, drains and monitors for the first 24 hours or so, but after that most should be removed and you will go back to the ward.

After five to ten days, you'll be able to go home and, around six to eight weeks later, you should be back to most of your normal activities. In other words, you can drive, go back to work provided it doesn't involve heavy manual labour and resume your sex life.

KEY POINTS

✓ Glyceryl trinitrate (GTN) taken as a tablet or spray under the tongue eases the pain of angina quickly, and should be carried at all times

✓ Other drugs, nitrates, beta-blockers and calcium channel blockers are very effective alone, and in combination, in controlling angina

✓ Angioplasty (PCI) is a technique where the narrowed artery is stretched by a high-pressure balloon, and is very effective in certain situations

✓ Coronary bypass surgery (CABG) is very effective in relieving angina and is particularly suitable for advanced disease

Treating a heart attack

If you have severe pain in the chest, feel cold, sweaty and nauseated, you are probably having a heart attack. This happens when a coronary artery becomes blocked, usually in an already narrowed vessel. The ambulance staff, paramedics or GP or a combination of all three may come to attend to you but their aims are the same: to stabilise your heart and reduce the amount of damage done to the muscle if at all possible.

When medical help arrives, you will be given oxygen via a facemask and have a plastic cannula (tube) inserted into a vein in your arm so that any drugs needed can go straight into your bloodstream. You will have ECG leads attached to your chest to monitor your heart rhythm and may be given morphine for the pain as well as something to stop the sickness.

DISSOLVING THE CLOT

In the early stages, the most important early treatment is with drugs to dissolve the clot and, in some cases, this may be started before you reach hospital. Although it may sound strange, chewing on

TREATMENT PRIORITIES

- Relieve pain and other symptoms, such as nausea
- Treat any serious cardiac irregularities promptly, with a defibrillator if necessary
- Restore blood supply to the affected heart muscle by dissolving the clot in the coronary artery
- Treat complications of the heart attack such as irregular heart beat or heart failure

an aspirin tablet is a good way to start. It is absorbed through the lining of the mouth and starts to thin the blood immediately.

In addition to aspirin, we have many new drugs available. The last 15 years have seen a dramatic change in the way we treat heart attacks because we now have powerful drugs which dissolve the clot that is at the root of the problem. These drugs are called thrombolytics (often referred to as 'clot-busters') and are given by injection. The most common one used in this country is streptokinase, but in some cases the more expensive tPa (tissue plasminogen activator) may be preferred.

The essential point about thrombolytics is that they work best if given within the first six hours after a heart attack. This is because, after this, the heart muscle may be too badly damaged even if the artery is unblocked again.

The use of these powerful drugs is not without some risk but large trials involving tens of thousands of patients with heart attacks have shown that the risks are greatly outweighed by the benefits. As thrombolytics dissolve blood clots they do make people more liable to bleed.

In some individuals, this may pose too great a risk – for instance, if someone has recently had a major operation, a stroke or a bleeding stomach ulcer. In these situations, it may be possible to undertake immediate angioplasty, if you are in

Thrombolytics given by injection   Thrombolytics dissolving clot

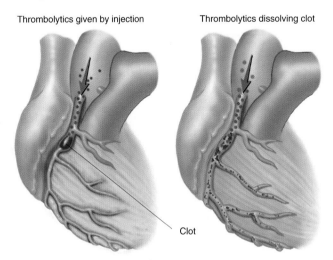

Clot

Effect of 'clot-buster' drugs on the clot in a heart attack: left before, and right after, giving thrombolytic drugs such as streptokinase or tPa.

STREPTOKINASE CARD

If you are given streptokinase, you will be given a card to show you have had it and when. This is because most people develop resistance to streptokinase after 5 days or so and this resistance lasts for a year or more. So if you need thrombolytic drugs within this period you will be given the alternative, tPa. It is very important that you carry this card with you at all times in case you are taken into hospital again.

a hospital where this is carried out (see page 48).

IRREGULAR HEART BEAT

In the early stages after a heart attack, the damaged heart muscle can become very irritable and produce irregular heart rhythms, some of which can cause the heart to stop completely. Sadly this is why some people die suddenly at home after developing chest pain before any help has arrived. These irregularities of heart rhythm – cardiac arrhythmias – can be treated very successfully by passing a brief electric shock through the heart using a gadget called a defibrillator – something you may well have seen on the TV or cinema screen.

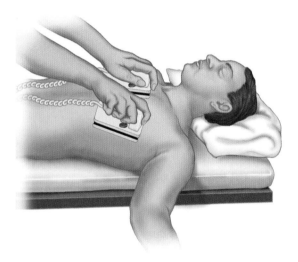

Use of cardiac defibrillator with the paddles placed on the chest.

People who need this treatment have always lost consciousness, so an anaesthetic is not necessary. Unfortunately, the procedure only works if the shock can be given within a few minutes of the heart stopping, which is why the 999 ambulance and paramedic service are so vital. You may be able to give vital help if you know what to do (see pages 74–5).

In hospital, people who have had a heart attack are usually treated in a special ward (the cardiac care unit) where the heart rhythms can be monitored closely for the first 24 or 48 hours – the danger period. If irregular rhythms start to develop they can usually be controlled with drug treatment and won't become severe enough to need a shock. After this the risk of rhythm problems becomes much less and drugs such as beta-blockers are used to prevent them happening again.

RECOVERING IN HOSPITAL

The worst period after a heart attack is the first day or two and, during this time, you will usually be monitored closely. After that most people have no more pain and are able to get up and about fairly quickly. After a straightforward heart attack, you may be able to go home after five to seven days, but some people, particularly elderly people, may need to stay in hospital longer.

In the first week, although there is no more pain, you may feel tired and have a slight temperature, but this feeling usually settles as the healing process begins. The damaged area of heart muscle is repaired and a scar forms just like any other part of the body after an injury. This scarring is more or less complete four to six weeks after the heart attack.

If this is the first time you have been in hospital or had anything seriously wrong, it may take some time to come to terms with what has happened, especially if you have financial and family commitments to worry about too. Nursing and medical staff are well aware of these worries and you should feel free to talk about them. It is time too to think about your lifestyle and what you can do to prevent another heart attack (see the section starting on page 66).

GOING HOME

After all the attention in hospital, it often feels strange to be going back home. You will naturally be worried about what you can and can't do, and your spouse or partner may be even more worried than you! In fact it is usually quite safe to do most things around the house, but any heavy physical activity should be avoided in the first few weeks. Remember that this includes some housework such as vacuum

Class of drug	Generic name*	Administration
Anti-platelet drugs	Aspirin Clopidogrel	Tablets Tablets
Nitrates	Glyceryl trinitrate Isosorbide dinitrate Isosorbide mononitrate Pentaerythritol tetranitrate	Under the tongue, in the cheek, tablets, skin patches, ointment or spray Tablets, capsules or under the tongue Tablets or capsules Tablets
Beta-blockers	Acebutolol Atenolol Bisoprolol Carvedilol Metoprolol Propranolol	Tablets or capsules Tablets or syrup Tablets Tablets Tablets Tablets or capsules
Calcium antagonists	Amlodipine Diltiazem Nicardipine Nifedipine Verapamil	Tablets Tablets or capsules Capsules Tablets or capsules Tablets or capsules
K+ channel activators	Nicorandil	Tablets
ACE inhibitors	Captopril Cilazapril Enalapril Fosinopril Lisinopril Perindopril Quinapril Ramipril Trandolapril	Tablets Tablets Tablets Tablets Tablets Tablets Tablets Capsules Capsules
Statins	Atorvastatin Fluvastatin Pravastatin Simvastatin	Tablets Capsules Tablets Tablets

* Pharmaceutical companies all give their products 'proprietary/trade' names as well as the
this on the package of your medication.

Purpose	Possible side effects
Thin blood	Gastric upset
Relieve angina	Flushing, headache
Slow heart rate, protect against heart attack	Tiredness, lethargy, cold hands, nightmares
Relieve angina	Flushing, headache, ankle swelling, constipation
Relieve angina	Headache, dizziness, vomiting
Protect against heart failure	Persistent dry cough, dizziness
Reduce cholesterol	Headache, indigestion, occasionally muscle inflammation

ctual 'generic/scientific' name. Only the generic name is listed here; you will be able to find cleaning, which uses more energy than you might think.

It is very important in these early stages that your family and friends try not to be too overprotective towards you. For them and for you, every little twinge of pain may become larger than life, and most people after a heart attack become much more aware of aches and pains that they would previously have ignored. Indeed it has been reported that 90 per cent of people experience some form of non-cardiac pain in the first few weeks after a heart attack.

However, about one in three people get angina, which may feel similar to a heart attack. It will usually come on with effort, and ease when you rest. If so, you should take the GTN which you will have been given in hospital. If the pain persists after using GTN, take another, and if it lasts more than 20 minutes you should get **immediate** medical advice. There may be a Helpline to the cardiac unit in your area and it is worth asking about this before you leave hospital.

TAKING MEDICINES WHEN YOU GO HOME

During the first week in hospital you will be given a number of different drugs, some to treat any compli-cations and others to reduce the risk of further problems over the next weeks and months.

There is now a wide variety of drugs that may be given to people who have had a heart attack, and your doctor will decide which ones will do you the most good. Don't be surprised if you know someone who has been given different treatment as drugs must be tailored to suit the needs of each individual.

• **Aspirin:** This is the most commonly prescribed drug, but some people can't take it, usually because they have stomach problems. Its main purpose is to reduce the stickiness of platelets – the cells in the blood which are involved in clotting. The new drug clopidrogel may now be an alternative.

• **Beta-blockers:** These are drugs that block the effect of adrenaline on receptors in the heart and blood vessels, thus reducing the risk of another heart attack and cutting the death rate. Many physicians prescribe them routinely after a heart attack but some people can't take them, for example, if they have asthma or bronchitis.

• **ACE inhibitors:** These have been a major advance in the treatment of heart problems. ACE – angiotensin-converting enzyme – increases the amount of angiotensin in the circulation. Angiotensin makes the blood vessels constrict and causes the body to retain more salt and water than normal. ACE inhibitors, by reducing the angiotensin levels, have cut the number of people developing heart attack and heart failure.

• **Statins:** These are potent new drugs which lower cholesterol. They act by reducing the amount of cholesterol that is made in the body, particularly in the liver and help to prevent arteries furring up any further (see page 68).

• **GTN:** This is one of the most important drugs you will be taking home, either as a spray or in tablet form. This is to use if you get any further pain in the chest after you leave hospital.

You should make sure you know how and when you should take GTN before you leave the hospital, and perhaps even try it so that you know what to expect. The doctors, nurses or pharmacist will answer your questions.

KEY POINTS

After a heart attack:

✓ Prompt treatment is vital; ring 999 rather than your GP

✓ Close monitoring is required in the first few days, usually in a cardiac care unit (CCU)

✓ Most people can expect to recover fully in six to eight weeks

✓ Drugs are important to prevent a recurrence

Getting over a heart attack

REHABILITATION

At one time doctors would have insisted you stay in bed for six to eight weeks after a heart attack in the mistaken belief that this would allow the heart to heal better. It was not surprising that after such a long period in bed people felt worse than they did before they had the attack. Things are very different now. Once the pain and general weakness have gone – usually a matter of a few days – the emphasis is on returning to normal over the next six to eight weeks.

Most hospitals now have a cardiac rehabilitation service – 'rehab' for short. The aims of cardiac rehabilitation are:

- Education: understanding the cause of the problem and how you are going to get better.

- Exercise: a graded exercise programme so that you can return to your normal activities.

- Prevention: how to avoid having a further heart attack.

The rehab programme usually begins in hospital when a nurse will visit you and try to answer some of the questions that must be troubling you and your family. You should be given some guidance about what sort of things you can and can't do when you leave hospital.

The exercise programme usually starts two to four weeks later and is supervised by a physiotherapist in the hospital gym. There will probably be a group of 10 to 15 other people going through the programme and it is a good time to talk together and share experiences. It is often very reassuring to see someone exercising quite energetically as they come to the end of the programme when you are just starting and worried about doing any exercise at all.

For many middle-aged people, this may be the first regular exercise they have done for years and so it will seem strange at first. However, most people find the exercise becomes easier and easier as the weeks go by and are likely to feel fitter at the end of the programme than they have done for years.

Rehabilitation sessions usually last one to two hours and take place about twice a week for six to eight weeks. As well as the exercise itself there is usually time to have some discussion about the cause of heart attacks and what can be done to prevent them.

There may also be visits from a pharmacist, a dietitian and a cardiologist to answer any questions you or your partner may have about your condition.

SPECIAL PROBLEMS

Driving

You are not allowed by law to drive your car for one month after a heart attack. You do not need to notify the DVLA but you should probably tell your insurance company. There are special regulations for people who drive for a living, such as bus drivers and lorry drivers, and you should discuss these problems with your doctor. In some towns these regulations also apply to taxi drivers as well.

Sexual activity

After a heart attack people worry about having sex. At first you don't usually feel like it but it is certainly reasonable to start sexual relations again three to four weeks after a heart attack if you want to. You should avoid being too vigorous until you feel fully recovered, which will normally be by about six to eight weeks. Some of the drugs you may be taking can reduce sex drive and if you feel this is the case you should have a word with your doctor.

Work

After a heart attack most people can go back to work after two or three months. For those with a physically undemanding job which does not involve much exercise eight weeks off work may be enough. For heavy manual workers longer may be necessary and special exercises are included in the exercise programme to build up your strength again. (Interestingly one of the first and most successful exercise programmes in Britain was in Barnsley to help miners get back to work.)

Holidays

For the first two or three months after a heart attack it is probably safest not to go abroad. Later you can probably travel where you like provided you have made a full recovery. If in doubt, discuss your plans with your doctor. You should always make sure that you are fully insured and that the policy does not exclude a heart condition! If you are on medication, make sure you have enough to last while you're away, and keep them in your hand luggage.

ANXIETY AND DEPRESSION

In the first few weeks after a heart attack, there are so many things going on and so much to think about that depression may not be obvious. However, once things start to get back to normal, you may have more time to worry about the future, and this is when problems can occur.

The most common reaction is a short temper, even in people who have been quite placid, and partners often complain that they get their 'head bitten off' for the slightest thing. These problems usually settle down if and when the person returns to work, and life starts getting back to normal, but some people continue to have a 'short fuse' for much longer.

Everyone worries after a heart attack and, despite all the positive advice from doctors, nurses and relatives, some people go on worrying. There is bound to be

some concern about having another heart attack, and all that it entails. It's natural to be worried about yourself and your family, even if it's difficult to put into words exactly why. A heart attack can be a real blow to your self-confidence, especially if you have never had any serious health problems before, and it's relatively easy to become depressed.

Recognising depression

Depression is just as much a real illness as heart disease, and also just as treatable. You may be depressed if you have several of the following symptoms:

* sadness or tearfulness
* loss of enjoyment or interest in work and hobbies
* low self-esteem
* preoccupation with your health
* poor concentration
* sleep disturbance, difficulty getting to sleep or waking early
* constant tiredness
* loss of interest in sex.

In depression, the levels of chemicals that transmit signals to the brain are abnormally low and treatment with antidepressants can bring them back to normal. These drugs are not addictive, unlike tranquillisers, and you will be able to stop taking them once you have fully recovered from depression.

Most people take them for three to six months.

The important thing about anxiety and depression is to realise that it is common and it can be helped. Often just discussing what you feel with someone else who has been through the same is all you need. Many towns now have a self-help group attached to the rehab service which gives long-term support where this is needed. If you have any of the symptoms listed on page 64, don't just struggle on waiting for them to go, but consult your doctor.

KEY POINTS

After a heart attack:

✓ Most problems occur in the first 48 hours; after that life soon returns to normal

✓ Regular exercise can help you to make a full recovery, but it should be supervised

✓ Emotional problems after a heart attack are common and can be helped by talking about them and sometimes by drugs

Look after your heart

You may think it is too late to think about prevention if you have already had a heart attack or developed angina. In fact, there are plenty of ways you can prevent the heart deteriorating further. There is a lot you can do to reduce your chances of having another heart attack by reducing your risk factors. This is especially important after bypass surgery as it means your new blood vessels will be less likely to fur up.

As we have already seen (pages 22–9), risk factors fall into two distinct categories: those over which you have no control and those that you can influence.

Other diseases, notably diabetes and hypertension (raised blood pressure), can increase the risk of developing CHD, but this risk is reduced if the conditions are well controlled with suitable medication.

RAISED CHOLESTEROL

Lipids is the collective term used by doctors to refer to fat-like substances in the blood. Cholesterol is the best known, but another type called triglycerides also plays a role in CHD.

Cholesterol has a bad reputation as a cause of disease of the heart and blood vessels, but in fact it also performs some essential functions in the body and no one could do without it entirely. It is manufactured in the liver and is used in the cell membranes, to make bile and to form vital chemical messengers (or hormones). Even if you excluded cholesterol completely from your diet, therefore, you would always have some in your blood.

In practice, most diets in Western countries include large amounts of animal fat which the body converts into cholesterol. These fats are absorbed by the stomach and intestines and passed to the liver, where they are broken down and circulated to the rest of the body to provide energy or to be stored in the fat cells. The fat circulates through the body in the blood in tiny particles containing mixtures of cholesterol and other fats.

When you have a blood cholesterol measurement, the laboratory will usually measure several other fats as well. The total cholesterol level is made up of two parts, called low-density lipoprotein (LDL) and high-density lipoprotein (HDL). LDL is the 'bad' cholesterol which, when the level is too high, builds up in the arterial wall to produce atheroma. About two-

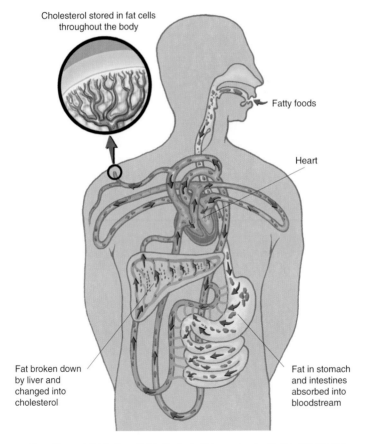

Cholesterol stored in fat cells throughout the body

Fatty foods

Heart

Fat broken down by liver and changed into cholesterol

Fat in stomach and intestines absorbed into bloodstream

Absorption and distribution of fat in the body. Fats are absorbed in the stomach and processed by the liver before being released into the circulation.

thirds of the cholesterol in the blood is LDL, and this is usually what doctors are referring to when they say you have a high cholesterol level.

HDL is, on the other hand, a 'good' cholesterol and the higher the level, the less likely you are to get heart disease. Women have a higher HDL level than men but this difference usually disappears after the menopause.

Triglycerides are the third type of fat measured in a blood sample. Triglycerides make up most of the fat in the fat cells of your body and, when released, provide the energy you need for everyday activities. Although triglycerides are not found in any quantity in the fatty deposits in arterial walls, high levels of triglycerides in the blood are indirectly linked to CHD.

Most people who have angina or a heart attack have high lipid levels, which are partly the result of what they eat and partly genetic. By careful dieting we can reduce lipid or cholesterol levels by 10–20 per cent but, if we want to lower them more than this, drugs are usually necessary.

You may find that your doctor prescribes more than one drug to lower lipids, as they work in different ways. However, you will also be given advice on reducing the amount of cholesterol in your diet as this is necessary if the drug treatment is to be fully effective (see pages 69–72).

Statins

The big change in the treatment of cholesterol in the last five years has been the development of this new class of drug which works by slowing the production of cholesterol in the liver. Statins are able to lower cholesterol by 20 to 30 per cent and have very few side effects.

There have now been several important studies, involving thousands of patients in Europe, Australia and the USA, showing that this reduction in cholesterol is followed by a 20 to 30 per cent reduction in the risk of further heart attacks. The most common statins used at present are simvastatin, atorvastatin and pravastatin, although there are many more being developed.

These drugs are usually taken as a single dose in the evening and have few side effects. Very occasionally they may cause inflammation in the muscles of the arms and legs, an aching that feels like 'flu. This occurs in the first few weeks after starting treatment and should be reported immediately to your doctor. It settles once the tablets are stopped.

If you have no problems with these drugs in the first few weeks you are unlikely to develop any after that.

Fibrates

For some individuals, particularly those with diabetes, the problem with the lipids may be not so much with cholesterol as with triglycerides, when another group of drugs called the fibrates may be used. They too may produce muscular pains in the first few weeks but otherwise have few side effects. They can reduce cholesterol levels by 10 to 15 per cent and cut the risk of CHD by about the same percentage.

Resins

Resins reduce cholesterol levels by binding cholesterol in the intestines and affecting their absorption into the body. These are taken in the form of a powder, usually in fruit juice, once or twice a day. As they are not absorbed into the body, they cannot cause any serious side effects in body tissues, but they can cause flatulence and belching or constipation in some people.

Resins too have been shown to reduce the risk of further heart attack, but they are less potent than the statins and reduce the risk by only 10 to 15 per cent.

DIET

Changing the sort of food that you have eaten all your life may not be easy but it is an important way to reduce the risk of further heart attack. The basic rules are fairly simple and given in the box on page 70.

Eating healthily doesn't mean giving up everything you enjoy or eating nothing but 'rabbit food'.

DRUG TREATMENT FOR RAISED CHOLESTEROL

Drug group	Examples of generic names	Example of trade names
statins	simvastatin	Zocor
	pravastatin	Lipostat
	fluvastatin	Lescol
	atorvastatin	Lipitor
fibrates	bezafibrate	Bezalip
	gemfibrozil	Lopid
resins	colestipol	Colestid
	cholestyramine	Questran

FOUR STEPS TO HEALTHY EATING

1 Cut down the total amount of fat in your diet
2 Replace animal fats (dairy fats) with vegetable oils
3 Eat more fresh fruit and vegetables
4 Go on a sensible weight-reducing diet if necessary

Most people in this country consume far more fat, and especially animal or dairy fat, than is good for them and cutting down would be a health bonus for your whole family. Red meat, hard cheeses, butter, cream, full-fat milk and yoghurt as well as cooking fats like lard are all high in so-called saturated fats. It is wise to cut down on saturated fats or just keep these foods for special occasions.

Certain foods, such as eggs, liver, kidney and shellfish, contain fairly high levels of cholesterol. You should restrict these to some extent. Although they probably contribute less to the level of blood cholesterol than foods high in animal fats.

In general, cutting down on fats is a good way to lose weight, and many people find that, after changing their diet, they also get much less indigestion. It's worth bearing in mind too that many processed and prepared foods such as pies, biscuits, cakes and so on may be high in animal fats as, of course, are burgers!

Now that we are all starting to become more health conscious, many foods in supermarkets are labelled to give us some idea of the fat content.

As well as reducing the overall amount of fat in your diet, you should try to use polyunsaturated fats – generally those from vegetable sources which are liquid at room temperature – or mono-unsaturated fat, like olive oil, whenever you can. If you are not sure which are the healthy oils, check the label or ask a dietitian as one or two vegetable oils are not good for the heart. Coconut oil in particular is almost as bad for the heart as pork dripping!

The other major change that will improve your diet from a health viewpoint is to eat as many pieces of fruit and vegetables as you can – at least five portions every day. If you can also increase your intake of other fibre-rich foods such as wholemeal bread, brown rice and pasta and breakfast cereals, especially oats, you will be well on the way to a diet that's good for

Healthy eating.

your overall health as well as your heart.

Fortunately the food industry is beginning to realise the importance of a healthy diet, and there are now many good recipe books to help, such as *Eating for your Heart's Delight* published by the British

Heart Foundation. What many writers ignore, however, is the higher cost of some healthy foods, and this often puts a strain on the family budget. If this is a real problem you should discuss the matter with your doctor. There may be benefits that you are entitled to, or a dietitian may be able to advise on the best way to budget the weekly shopping.

SMOKING

The benefits of stopping smoking are real and start from the day you give up and, five years on, your risk of having another heart attack will be halved. You do have to stop completely, however: cutting down or changing from cigarettes to cigars or a pipe does little to reduce the risk.

Doctors themselves realised this 30 years ago when the research linking heart disease and smoking was first published. Until then, doctors were among the heaviest smokers, but now there are very few indeed.

Many people find it easy to stop smoking in hospital, but it's much harder to keep it up when you go home. If you have smoked since you were a teenager it can be a real problem. This is where all the family can help, because there is nothing worse when the craving is there than for your partner or daughter to light up. Hospitals are now 'no smoking' areas and your home should be too!

What is the best way of giving up? That's going to be different for everyone. Some people have found it easiest to stop suddenly. Others prefer to stop gradually, perhaps cutting down by a cigarette a day over several weeks. Part of the problem is an addiction to nicotine itself, and for some the use of nicotine chewing gum or skin patches can be a great help.

Sometimes talking to others trying to give up is the best help, and many hospitals and health centres run 'stopping smoking' sessions. Some even swear by hypnosis – as doctors we don't care so long as you kick the habit!

One of the things that often puts people – especially women – off giving up smoking is the tendency to put on weight afterwards. We are still not sure

why this happens. Certainly the appetite improves, and some people take to eating sweets to reduce their craving for a cigarette. On average most people put on between half and one stone in the first six months after stopping smoking. However, if you change to a healthier, low-fat diet at the same time the extra weight usually comes off again gradually over the next six to twelve months.

A new drug bupropion (Zyban) has received a great deal of publicity because it can be very effective in helping patients to give up smoking. It is not suitable for everyone, however; consult your doctor if in doubt.

STRESS

When you develop angina or have had a heart attack, it is an opportunity to weigh up the priorities in your life. You may feel that a job which has occupied a large proportion of your time and energy over the years now seems less important to you than your family and friends and your other interests. Although there is no scientific proof that changing the way you live reduces your risk, it will certainly improve the quality of your life.

PROTECTIVE FACTORS

Alcohol

There has been quite a lot of publicity recently about the good effects of alcohol when taken in moderation. Of course, high levels of alcohol taken on a regular basis can poison the heart as well as other internal organs such as the brain and the liver.

So what is moderation? The amount of alcohol that seems to be good for you is around two to three units a day, with women sticking to the lower end of the range. A unit is a measure of spirits, glass of wine or half a pint of beer or cider. Although it was first thought that red wine was particularly good at preventing heart attacks, it now seems that in fact any form of alcohol has the same effect.

Exercise

Regular exercise is also good for you and can protect against CHD. There have been many studies in the USA and Europe which show that, if you take regular exercise (20 minutes two or three times a week), this reduces the risk of CHD when compared with the 'couch potatoes' of this world.

If you've actually had a heart attack, you will be taught about exercise in your rehabilitation sessions, but in fact anyone who has any form of CHD may well need more exercise too. If you have never exercised before and are unsure how to start, do ask your doctor's advice.

What type of exercise you go for

is probably not important providing it stimulates the heart and circulation sufficiently. You should do what you like best: walking, swimming, jogging, exercising in the gym or even dancing are all likely to help. Most people will need to start relatively slowly and build up to longer and more strenuous sessions gradually. If you go to a gym or an exercise class, you should be shown how to warm up properly before and afterwards, and it's a good idea to get into the habit of doing this with any exercise session.

The idea of 'going for the burn'– exercising until it hurts and beyond – has been thoroughly discredited. If you feel pain, dizziness or find it hard to breathe, stop and rest and have a break from exercise if you are injured or not feeling well.

WORKING WITH YOUR DOCTOR

Although smoking and exercise levels are major risk factors which are to a large extent under your own control, there are other spheres where you and your doctor will need to work together to minimise the risk of further problems. People with conditions that make CHD more likely, such as diabetes and hypertension (high blood pressure), need to try to keep these under good control by regular checks at the surgery (see pages 27–9).

Hypertension
Make a big effort to take your tablets regularly, even though you have no symptoms. See your doctor for regular blood pressure checks.

Diabetes
Try to keep your weight as close as possible to what it should be for your height.

Do your best to keep your blood glucose levels within the normal range by paying careful attention to your diet and taking your prescribed treatment properly. Exercise is important because it helps to reduce your weight and also reduces your insulin requirement.

Raised lipid levels
Make an effort to stick to your diet, take any tablets correctly and attend for regular blood tests.

WHAT TO DO IN AN EMERGENCY
A heart attack can happen anywhere; everyone should know what to do to help someone if they collapse and the heart stops beating. Basic life support (BLS) is not difficult and it may be literally life saving to learn how to do it.

Instructors are available in most towns, from voluntary agencies such as the St John's Ambulance or from the local hospital. If you or someone with you develops chest pain which seems similar to the heart pain associated with an earlier heart attack, there are some basic steps to follow:

- Rest sitting or lying down
- Take GTN medicine and wait for five minutes
- If the pain is still as bad or worse after five to ten minutes, take a second dose
- If this has no effect, telephone for an ambulance
- Chew on an aspirin (unless you or the person concerned is known to be allergic to it) as this will start to thin the blood and discourage clots.

WHAT TO DO IN AN EMERGENCY – ABC

Airway: ensure that there is nothing preventing air getting in through the nose and mouth

Breathing: see whether there is any spontaneous breathing

Circulation: feel for a pulse in the neck

If there is no breathing and you can't feel the pulse, a cardiac arrest has probably occurred. Call for help and, if you know how, start mouth-to-mouth respiration and cardiac massage.

KEY POINTS

✓ Changing to a healthy diet improves your fitness

✓ Drug treatment to lower cholesterol reduces the risk of CHD

✓ Stopping smoking reduces your risk further and is effective immediately

✓ Regular exercise improves the state of your heart and circulation

Useful addresses

Blood Pressure Association
60 Cranmer Terrace
London SW17 0QS
Tel: 020 8772 4994
Fax: 020 8772 4999
Website: www.bpassoc.org.uk

Raises public awareness about,and offers information and support to, people affected by high blood pressure and health care professionals. Has a wide selection of literature and membership scheme.

British Heart Foundation
14 Fitzhardinge Street
London W1H 6DH
Tel: 020 7935 0185
Fax: 020 7486 5820
Helpline: 08450 708070
Website: www.bhf.org.uk

Funds research, promotes education and raises money to buy equipment to treat heart disease. Information and support available for people with heart conditions. Via Heartstart UK arranges training in emergency life-saving techniques for lay people.

Coronary Prevention Group
London School of Hygiene and Tropical Medicine
2 Taviton Street
London WC1H 0BT
Tel: 020 7927 2125
Fax: 020 7927 2127
Email: cpg@lshtm.ac.uk
Website: www.healthnet.org.uk

First British charity devoted to the prevention of coronary heart disease. For information booklets please send s.a.e.

Diabetes UK
10 Parkway
London NW1 7AA
Tel: 020 7424 1000
Fax: 020 7424 1001
Email: info@diabetes.org.uk
Helpline: 020 7424 1030
Website: www.diabetes.org.uk
Textline 020 7424 1888

Provides advice and information for

people with diabetes and their families. Has local support groups.

Health Development Agency
Trevelyan House
30 Great Peter Street
London SW1P 2HW
Helpline: 0800 555 777
Website: www.hda-online.org.uk

Formerly the Health Education Authority; now deals only with research. Publications on health matters can be ordered via helpline.

Heart UK
7 North Road
Maidenhead
Berks SL6 1PE
Tel: 01628 628638
Fax: 01628 628698
Email: ask@heartuk.org.uk
Website: www.heartuk.org.uk

Offers information, advice and support to people with coronary heart disease and especially those at high risk of familial hypercholesterolaemia. Members receive bi-monthly magazine. Recently merged with British Hyperlipidaemia Association.

Resuscitation Council (UK)
5th Floor, Tavistock House North
Tavistock Square
London WC1H 9HR
Tel: 020 7388 4678
Fax: 020 7383 0773
Email: enquiries@resus.org.uk
Website: www.resus.org.uk

Set standards and run courses for health care professionals. Fund research.

Smoking Quitlines (Quit)
211 Old Street
London EC1V 9NR
Tel: 020 7251 1551
Fax: 020 7251 1661
Email: reception@quit.org.uk
Helpline: 0800 002200
Website: www.quit.org.uk
Offers advice on giving up smoking.
Separate helplines for:
N. Ireland: 02890 663281
Scotland: 0800 848484
Wales: 0800 169 0169 (NHS Smoking Helpline)

THE INTERNET AS A SOURCE OF FURTHER INFORMATION
After reading this book, you may feel that you would like further information on the subject. One source is the internet and there are a great many websites with useful information about medical disorders, related charities and support groups. Some websites, however, have unhelpful and inaccurate information. Many are sponsored by commercial organisations or raise revenue by advertising, but nevertheless aim to provide impartial and trustworthy health information. Others may be reputable but you should be aware that they may be biased in their recommendations. Remember that treatment advertised on international websites may not be available in the UK.

Unless you know the address of the specific website that you want to visit (for example familydoctor.

co.uk), you may find the following guidelines helpful when searching the internet.

There are several different sorts of websites that you can use to look for information, the main ones being search engines, directories and portals.

Search engines and directories

There are many search engines and directories that all use different algorithms (procedures for computation) to return different results when you do a search. Search engines use computer programs called spiders, which crawl the web on a daily basis to search individual pages within a site and then queue them ready for listing in their database.

Directories, however, consider a site as a whole and use the description and information that was provided with the site when it was submitted to the directory to decide whether a site matches the searcher's needs. For both there is little or no selection in terms of quality of information, although engines and directories do try to impose rules about decency and content. Popular search engines in the UK include:

google.co.uk
aol.co.uk
msn.co.uk
lycos.co.uk

hotbot.co.uk
overture.com
ask.co.uk
espotting.com
looksmart.co.uk
alltheweb.com
uk.altavista.com

The two biggest directories are:

yahoo.com
dmoz.org

Portals

Portals are doorways to the internet that provide links to useful sites, news and other services, and may also provide search engine services (such as msn.co.uk). Many portals charge for putting their clients' sites high up in your list of search results. The quality of the websites listed depends on the selection criteria used in compiling the portal, although portals focused on a specific group, such as medical information portals, may have more rigorous inclusion criteria than other searchable websites. Examples of medical portals can be found at:

nhsdirect.nhs.uk
patient.co.uk

Links to many British medical charities will be found at the Association of Medical Research Charities (www.amrc.org.uk) and Charity Choice (www.charitychoice.co.uk).

Search phrases

Be specific when entering a search phrase. Searching for information on 'cancer' could give astrological information as well as medical: 'lung cancer' would be a better choice. Either use the engine's advanced search feature and ask for the exact phrase, or put the phrase in quotes – 'lung cancer' – as this will link the words. Adding 'uk' to your search phrase will bring up mainly British websites, so a good search would be 'lung cancer' uk (don't include uk within the quotes).

Always remember that the internet is international and unregulated. Although it holds a wealth of invaluable information, individual websites may be biased, out of date or just plain wrong. Family Doctor Publications accepts no responsibility for the content of links published in their series.

Index